VEGETARIAN SOUL FOOD COOKBOOK

VEGETARIAN
SOUL
FOOD
COOKBOOK

75 CLASSIC RECIPES TO SATISFY YOUR CRAVINGS

ALEXIA WILKERSON

Photography by Annie Martin

ROCKRIDGE
PRESS

Interior and Cover Designer: Linda Snorina
Art Producer: Alyssa Williams
Editor: Leah Zarra
Production Editor: Rachel Taenzler
Production Manager: Riley Hoffman

Photography © 2021 Annie Martin. Food styling by Nadine Page.

Paperback ISBN: 978-1-64876-750-0
eBook ISBN: 978-1-64876-751-7
R0

CONTENTS

COLLARD PILAU, 90

INTRODUCTION

I was born and raised in North Carolina with a large family. Sunday dinners, holidays, and family get-togethers played an important role in our lives. They were a time for the whole family to help in the kitchen, cooking the soul food recipes that had been passed down through generations for hundreds of years. This is what making soul food is all about: strengthening family connections and using traditional recipes to bring comfort and build community.

As a child, I loved my grandmother's homemade dumplings and soup recipes, which had been passed down by *her* grandmother, who was born in the late 1800s. Every New Year's Day we made collard greens and corn bread, a combination that is said to bring good luck for the upcoming year. As a child, I never questioned why these foods were lucky; I just followed instructions in the kitchen and enjoyed cooking with my family. As an adult, I understand that collard greens represent money and corn bread represents gold, and I feel proud knowing that I am upholding our family traditions and maintaining that connection to my ancestors.

Today, a lot of people are concerned with their diets and developing healthy eating habits. Many are turning to a partial or fully vegetarian diet, both for its health benefits as well as ethical considerations. As a result, Southern comfort foods and traditional soul foods from the Deep South are eaten less frequently. Admittedly, they can be filled with sugar, fat, and meats, and may be considered unhealthy. But to me, the essence, flavors, and traditions of soul food are not completely incompatible with healthy eating and are certainly not incompatible with vegetarian eating. And this book is my proof.

So, whether you just want to incorporate a few meatless meals here and there, or you are following a strict vegetarian diet every day, you don't have to write soul food off. This book will teach you how to make soul food (often) healthy and (always) meatless without sacrificing flavor. Plus, I've designed these recipes to provide quick and easy versions of all your favorite soul food classics.

Throughout the following pages, I will discuss the history of soul food and its relationship to Southern cuisine and cover the basics of setting up a vegetarian kitchen. You'll learn ways to prepare quick soul foods that feel good and taste delicious. I'll also give you some kitchen tips, and suggest what to stock up on to make these meatless classics with a twist. If you have a little bit of time, patience, and love, you are already well on your way to bringing some soul food into your own kitchen.

CHAPTER 1

VEGETARIAN SOUL FOOD

This chapter explores the history of soul food and the philosophy of how to adapt it to fit a vegetarian diet. It will cover the basics of soul food cooking and what you'll need to set up your kitchen to make vegetarian cooking as easy as possible. We'll also break down some of the main ingredients used in traditional soul food recipes and discuss workable vegetarian swaps.

◄ VEGGIE-FULL POT PIE, 70

WHAT IS SOUL FOOD?

Soul food, or the cooking and eating of soul food, dates back hundreds of years and has deep roots that connect Black Americans to their ancestors. The term "soul food" can be interpreted differently, depending on who you ask. In its simplest form, soul food is a style of food stemming from the rural South and primarily cooked in the Deep South—the states in the southeastern part of the country, from Texas to South Carolina, Alabama to Florida—for holidays, family reunions, birthdays, church get-togethers, and especially Sunday meals. Yet despite the perception that soul food is innately American cuisine, it is actually a fusion of European, African, and Native American ingredients and cooking techniques that are rooted in the time of the Transatlantic Slave Trade when enslaved individuals were brought to the Americas and the Caribbean. Soul food is built upon ingredients that were traditionally considered less desirable: the only ingredients available to enslaved cooks. The ingredients were either rationed to them by slave owners, brought with them from Africa and planted in America, or learned about and adapted from Native Americans. Making these humble ingredients into delicious dishes for the entire family is the essence of soul food.

Soul food dishes are known to have a variety of side options, like black-eyed peas, corn bread, macaroni and cheese, grits, and collard greens. Main protein options traditionally have included fried or barbecued pork, chicken, and fish. The use of pork bits and lard is common for adding richness and flavor as well as extra spice to add complexity to dishes. Most enslaved people needed to eat a diet high in calories in order to endure the physical labor demanded of them, which led to frying and breading many of the foods. In soul food, many of the techniques and ingredients have significance both historically and regionally; when you look at the history, you can begin to grasp the complexity of what is considered soul food, why it is sometimes hard to define, and how it is so entwined with the cultures and the families from which it blossomed.

Soul food tends to stay consistent throughout the South—lots of greens like collards and turnips, lots of cornmeal, and lots of sweet potatoes—and doesn't have regional variations like other types of cuisine tend to have. Instead, soul food recipes get their slight variations from families and individual taste preferences, many of which are considered to be "secret" family recipes that are passed down from generation to generation. The variations in recipes are more personal as people focus on mastering the best type of spice blends, cooking techniques, and ingredient ratios to set their recipe apart from other forms of the same dish.

Origins

Soul food is built upon the resourcefulness of enslaved people. It uses the ingredients once afforded to enslaved cooks, the foods that the slave owners themselves did not want. For instance, enslaved people were often given a "peck" of cornmeal as a large part of their rations. They began looking to Native American cooking techniques to learn how to use cornmeal in different ways; this is where corn bread, grits, and the use of cornmeal in various soul food recipes is rooted.

Although they received scarce food rations from slave owners, enslaved people were also able to garden, so they began planting what they knew: their native foods that they brought with them to America. Soul food ingredients like okra, black-eyed peas, watermelon, and yams were brought to America from West Africa. Along with ingredients, cooking techniques during slavery were influenced by African and Native American methods, most notably cooking over an open flame and cooking in large batches for family-style eating.

Before emancipation, recipes were passed from generation to generation orally. After emancipation in the 1860s, African American cooks traveled across the nation, many of them taking jobs as cooks in white households (in the White House, in fact) or in restaurants. In fact, soul food restaurants were some of the first Black-owned businesses in the North. They brought their recipes with them as a piece of home, a piece of their history, and a piece of their families. As they fused the recipes they'd used during slavery with other American foods, their recipes became part of the African American culture known today as soul food. But although ingredients like black-eyed peas and collard greens were historically considered less desirable, the recipes that cooks created from them were just the opposite. They were infused with love, soul, creativity, and flavor and were ultimately passed down from generation to generation, putting the "soul" in soul food.

It wasn't until decades after slavery ended in the United States that the term "soul food" was coined to describe a style of cooking. Following the rise of soul music in the 1940s, the term "soul" began to be associated with African American culture, and eventually the term "soul food" arose during the Black Power Movement in the 1960s when there was a strong call to embrace African American history and culture.

Soul Food versus Southern Food

Many cooks will tell you that all soul food is Southern food, but not all Southern food is soul food. Other cooks will tell you that Southern food is the mother cuisine giving birth to soul food, along with Cajun and Creole food, etc. In other words, soul food is simply one type of Southern food. That's because soul food stemmed from Southern food but has notable differences. Southern food refers more to any cooking style originating in the South and can vary based on region and state, and soul food tends to stay consistent regardless of region.

For instance, Cajun food and Creole food, which are both types of Southern food, have slight variations based on the cooking styles of original settlers in Louisiana. Creole food is historically known to be influenced by wealthy European settlers who migrated to New Orleans and used more refined ingredients, and Cajun food came from French settlers in the Southwest Louisiana countryside where they used more rustic ingredients. Other regional variations of Southern food include Floribbean, Gullah, and Low Country foods. Floribbean is a mixture of Cuban, Haitian, and Spanish cuisines that is consumed mostly in the south of Florida. Gullah cuisine comes from the coastal districts of South Carolina, Georgia, and Northeast Florida and is very similar to West African cuisine, utilizing seafood, rice, and lots of vegetables. Low Country cuisine originates in the coastal plains of South Carolina and features many seafood and rice dishes as well.

Unlike the broad umbrella of Southern food, soul food tends to remain consistent across African American communities all over the country, with dishes like black-eyed peas and corn bread, shrimp and grits, hush puppies, and collard greens being standard fare no matter the region. The real difference between Southern and soul food may be more elusive. You will hear many cooks say that love, family, faith, and being able to escape from the stresses of everyday life over a nice meal is what truly distinguishes soul food.

Styles and Methods

Soul food cooking style embraces the use of time-honored ingredients and cooking techniques. Food was traditionally made in large quantities for large groups of people and the emphasis today remains on cooking soul food for large family celebrations or Sunday church gatherings. Despite their distinctions, many of the cooking methods commonly used in soul food are the same ones you'll find in other types of Southern cooking, including barbecuing, stewing, smoking, and deep-frying. Each of these techniques is particularly useful for preparing the types of foods that were historically available to enslaved and impoverished cooks: Smoking and barbequing help soften tougher cuts of meat, and deep frying adds flavor and texture to otherwise bland foods. Stewing makes leafy vegetables more digestible and allows you to make soups from a variety of scrap ingredients. Slow cooking is another type of stewing method that is associated with

Southern and soul food. The rise of crock pots has modernized this traditional cooking method, making some soul food dishes far more accessible and easier to create with the simplicity of a one-pot, no-hassle meal.

Making Soul Food Meatless

When it comes to soul food recipes, going meatless isn't as difficult as you might think. After all, some of the most common ingredients in soul food include greens, sweet potatoes, black-eyed peas, rice, and corn—all vegetarian-friendly. Plus, soul food stems, in large part, from Western and Central Africa, where it is reported that many of the tribes enjoyed a plant-based diet. A lot of the traditional dishes are already vegetable-heavy, and many that do have meat include just a bit of pork or fat to add richness. Simply substituting other flavorful ingredients allows you to easily create vegetarian versions of popular soul food staples.

Here is my philosophy about making these dishes meatless: I hope to accommodate a large percentage of people who are already following, or would like to follow, an entirely or partially vegetarian lifestyle. My approach is to offer tasty meatless recipes that are not repetitive or boring and do not compromise the great taste and essence of soul food. For instance, fried chicken may be difficult to envision without the meat; my goal, however, is to prove to you that the veggie alternative does not compromise on great taste and texture (see Fried Mushroom "Chicken," page 74).

And I do keep health in mind. Although enslaved people required diets high in calories and fat, we live differently today and have different needs from our foods. Traditional soul food dishes heavy on the pork and beef can contribute to high blood pressure, heart disease, and many other health issues. Offering meatless alternatives to these soul food meals promotes heart health, reduces cancer risk, and decreases obesity, which has its own numerous risks. That said, a vegetarian diet is not necessarily a healthier diet in and of itself.

Does Vegetarian Equal Healthy?

Vegetarian diets do typically lead to healthier eating habits, but not all vegetarian dishes are inherently healthy; you still have to be smart about your ingredient choices. Butter, cheeses, heavy creams, sugar, refined wheat, and oils are vegetarian but would not necessarily fall into the healthier eating category. When eaten in abundance, even without meat, they can compromise your health.

For this book, I've developed meat-free versions of soul food favorites, as well as modern twists on the classics that enhance their flavor. I've also intentionally focused on creating some dishes that are a bit healthier (less sugar, less butter, less fried, etc.) than their original counterparts. Nonetheless, some of the classic recipes are a bit heavier; I did not want to compromise taste and tradition by straying too far from their true essence. These dishes should be enjoyed in moderation.

A VEGETARIAN SOUL FOOD KITCHEN

Cooking vegetarian soul food may sound daunting at first, but when you have the right ingredients and tools in your kitchen, it's actually quite easy. Here we'll cover the basics of putting together a vegetarian kitchen, so you'll be ready to get cooking soul food in no time.

Soul Food Staples

Many of the ingredients used throughout this book can be found very affordably at your local grocery store, though if you're new to making soul food it's possible you haven't noticed them before (i.e., collard greens, okra). Here are some of the most important ingredients used in traditional soul food cooking, along with the vegetarian ingredients needed to substitute for traditional meats.

SPICES

Spices have played a major role in soul food cooking because they helped boost the flavors of ingredients that were considered to be less desirable. Here, without meat, these spices play an even more important role in elevating the dishes. A spiced dish adds layers of complexity and flavor, taking it from bland to exciting.

Smoked paprika, onion powder, thyme, bay leaves, garlic, vegetable bouillon (in a paste or cube), **Cajun seasoning, hot pepper sauce,** and **cayenne pepper** are some of the staples. **Liquid smoke** is a flavor additive used as an alternative to cooking with wood smoke. It maintains the same aroma and taste of wood smoke and is used to save time instead of barbecuing or smoking ingredients. Dried herbs and spices are popular in soul food cooking because they are generally less expensive and more potent than fresh so you don't need as much in a recipe.

COOKING FROM SCRATCH AND SHORTCUTS

Because soul food recipes are generally passed down through a family for generations, many are made from scratch. But soul food, at its core, stems from a combination of cooking from scratch and using shortcuts. Due to the unfortunate circumstances that were present when soul food first came about, people had no choice but to use what was available to them. As these shortcuts developed, they, too, were passed down throughout generations. Cooking with the shortcuts of the day is actually an integral part of soul food cooking. Current shortcuts include things like precut or frozen vegetables, canned beans, store-bought barbecue sauce, store-bought tomato juice, and premade vegetable stock; they make soul food cooking more accessible and easier to prepare. Dried herbs and spices are another shortcut commonly used in soul food. Because dried herbs and spices are usually less expensive (and more potent) than buying them fresh, the use of dried herbs and spices is more common in soul food dishes. They are more affordable and can be used in smaller quantities.

Although shortcuts are great and used frequently in soul food cooking, certain things are just worth the extra time spent preparing from scratch, such as making mashed potatoes fresh instead of using a box. And when it comes to biscuits, breads, and cakes, they are, and probably always will be, cooked completely from scratch. That's where love is truly put into the dishes: the process.

A note on fake meat alternatives/shortcuts: Many restaurants and fast-food establishments are offering fake meat alternatives like the Impossible Foods or Beyond Meat brands, for example, that are indeed plant-based products designed to look, smell, and taste like meat. Here, I've avoided this costly and inconsistently tasty faux meat trend. I recommend tofu and tempeh minimally and have focused instead on healthy, fresh ingredients as substitutes for meat.

Cabbage is used in a variety of recipes as a side dish on its own or incorporated into soups. Sautéed Seasoned Cabbage (page 44), Coleslaw from Scratch (page 38), and Cabbage Soup with Veggies (page 54) are just some of the soul food recipes that use this versatile, ubiquitous, and inexpensive ingredient.

Corn is used in a variety of dishes, such as Honey Butter Corn Bread (page 94), creamed corn, corn casseroles, soups, and stews. You can use canned corn as a shortcut in some recipes, but freshly cut corn off of the cob will give you the best flavor. Enslaved cooks, who received cornmeal as a part of their rations from slaveowners, learned various techniques to cook with corn from the Native Americans.

Greens (collards, turnip, and dandelion) were considered to be less desirable ingredients in antebellum times, so they were available to enslaved cooks who took these undesirables and made them delicious. They are popular cooked as a side dish (see Vegan Collard Greens, page 34) or added to soups and stews (see Eat Your Collard Greens Soup, page 66). They are traditionally sautéed with onions, spices, pork bits, and lard, but here I omit the pork fat and use vegetable broth instead. And did you know that dandelions are reported to have multiple health benefits, ranging from reducing cancer risk to providing multiple vitamins and antioxidants?

Okra was originally imported from Africa into the United States and the Caribbean during the time of the Transatlantic Slave Trade. It is typically stewed in gumbo (see Okra Gumbo Remix, page 63) or cut into small pieces and fried until it's crunchy and satisfying (see Traditional Fried Okra, page 40). Most grocery stores carry fresh okra in the vegetable aisles (especially in summer, when it's in season), and it's typically stored near the chile peppers and bell peppers. If you can't find fresh okra, look for it frozen; you can usually find it both whole and sliced.

Russet potatoes are used in a variety of soup and stew recipes and are the main ingredient in dishes like mashed potatoes, hash browns, Potato Cakes (page 30), and breakfast potatoes (see Fried Potato and Onion Medley, page 20).

Sweet potato is one of the most popular ingredients in soul food dishes. Its popularity probably stems from the fact that West Africans grew and ate yams (quite similar to sweet potatoes) in Africa prior to and during the slave trade. They are delicious and nutrient dense, full of antioxidants, protein, and beta-carotene. They are also versatile. They can be candied, chopped into cubes for a hash, or smashed for a Sweet Potato French Toast Casserole (page 24). And of course, the age-old favorite: Sweet Potato Pie (see Sumptuous

Sweet Potato Pie, page 111). If you don't have time to cook potatoes from scratch, you can use canned sweet potatoes in some recipes without affecting the final flavor of the dish.

Tomatoes were used by enslaved chefs who were sometimes permitted to plant small vegetable gardens to supplement their rations. They are often used in stews and gumbo today, mostly in canned form. Green tomatoes are used for the popular classic Fried Green Tomatoes (page 48).

FRUITS

Apples can be used in both breakfast and dessert dishes, from apple-cinnamon pancakes and Old-Fashioned Cinnamon Apple Oatmeal (page 28) to Cozy Apple Cobbler (page 106) or pie.

Peaches and blackberries are popular fruits for cobblers and pies (see Soulful Peach Cobbler, page 112). Fresh fruit is preferred over frozen if possible. If you do use frozen fruit, make sure to defrost it before using in recipes to prevent them from turning out too watery.

BEANS, LEGUMES, AND NUTS

Black-eyed peas were brought over by enslaved individuals from Africa. They are a staple of soul food, most commonly served alongside corn bread and stewed with onions (see Lucky Black-Eyed Peas, page 43).

Green beans are a popular soul food side dish when sautéed with onions and spicy seasonings (see Sautéed Green Beans, page 49).

Kidney beans are used for chili and some other dishes, most commonly soups or stews (see Red Beans and Rice Mélange, page 76).

Pecans are native to North America and were first grown along the Mississippi River and into Alabama before being brought to Georgia to be commercially harvested. Pecan pie (see Impeccable Pecan Pie, page 109) and praline candies are popular throughout Southern and soul food recipes.

Pinto beans are also used in chili and are called for in Pinto Bean Soup (page 59).

Cane sugar is used to sweeten fruit to make cobblers and is often mixed with cinnamon to create a cinnamon-sugar blend that pairs deliciously with apples and oatmeal dishes. Once cane sugar production was brought to the South, it began to replace maple sugar in recipes because of its convenience. After the abolishment of slavery, however, the production of cane sugar reduced significantly and maple sugar made a comeback.

Corn syrup is used as a sweet and thickening sauce for recipes like my Impeccable Pecan Pie (page 109).

Honey is frequently used to create a sweet crust in corn bread recipes (see Honey Corn Bread Waffle, page 21). It can be mixed with butter and is often drizzled over biscuits. Honey can be a hot topic in the vegan world because it is an animal by-product. If you are vegan, you can use agave syrup instead.

Molasses, one of the items sometimes rationed to enslaved chefs, is a heavy, sweet syrup that gets its golden color from caramelizing sugar. It can be used to sweeten barbecue sauce and baked beans. I always prefer to make my own molasses (see Mom's Homemade Molasses, page 100) because it has a superior flavor, but if you don't have time, look for Grandma's or Brer Rabbit brands in grocery stores. You can find them in the baking aisles close to corn syrup and other sweeteners.

Pure maple syrup is a breakfast staple used on pancakes and waffles and is also an ingredient used to sweeten recipes (see Candied Yams, page 35). Maple syrup originated in the Northern states and was introduced by Native Americans.

Sorghum syrup is another popular sugar substitute used in various soul food recipes. The sorghum plant arrived in the American South as part of the African slave trade. It is a tall grass with a sweet sap that was developed as a sugar and molasses alternative.

PANTRY

Apple cider vinegar adds the tang to coleslaw, baked beans, and barbecue sauces (see Coleslaw from Scratch, page 38). Apple cider vinegar is sweeter and more palatable than regular white vinegar, so is a better choice for flavor development. This vinegar will last for 2 years unopened and 1 year after opening.

Baking powder leavens recipes, but is used to lighten the texture of baked goods.

Baking soda leavens baked goods to help them rise and get fluffy.

Cornmeal is used to make corn bread (see Hot Water Corn Bread, page 95), Hush Puppies (page 99), and Johnny Cakes or "hoecakes" (see page 26). It can be stored in an airtight container for up to a year.

Cornstarch is used to help thicken sauces.

Grits are a Southern staple eaten as a side dish similar to mashed potatoes or as a breakfast option similar to oatmeal (see Creamy Stone-Ground Grits, page 18). Grits are made with finely ground white corn.

Heavy (whipping) cream adds extra creaminess to recipes like Creamy Stone-Ground Grits (page 18) and Hearty Potato Soup (page 56).

Mayonnaise is a staple pantry ingredient used in many creamy recipes like Creamy Potato Salad (page 46) and Coleslaw from Scratch (page 38). There are healthier varieties of mayonnaise that can be used for some of the recipes.

Oils and fats such as vegetable oils, butter, coconut oil, canola oil, olive oil, and grapeseed oil are all great vegetarian options to use in place of traditional lard. Olive oil is used primarily throughout the recipes in the book. Canola oil and vegetable oil are frequently used for frying or grilling.

Rice is used to make the Red Beans and Rice Mélange (page 76), and is also typically used in gumbo or served beneath hearty stews. There are a variety of different rice types available at the market; long-grain white rice is the kind used in Southern cuisine. Sometimes I replace it with brown rice or wild rice for a healthier alternative. Rice will last for years, if stored properly in airtight containers.

Southern flour, like the White Lily brand, is made with Southern wheat, which contains less protein than other flours. The lower protein when mixed with gluten creates a soft, fluffy reaction upon baking, which is great for biscuits. Southern flour and self-rising flours are often used in soul food recipes over all-purpose flours (such as Grandma's Biscuits, page 19). Flour has a long shelf life and typically lasts anywhere from 3 to 8 months once opened if stored in a sealed container.

Vegetable stock or broth, in liquid form or dried powder cubes, is used to add flavor in place of traditional chicken or beef stock. It is mostly used in soup and stew recipes but also in recipes like Brown Gravy Extraordinaire (page 101).

Kitchen Equipment

Having the proper tools in your kitchen will help make your cooking stress-free and enjoyable. In this section, you'll find information about the best equipment for preparing vegetarian and soul food meals, as well as some additional tools that are nice to have and, although not essential, will help simplify the cooking process.

ESSENTIALS

Box graters are great (no pun intended) for grating cheese or grating potatoes for hash browns, and are a fun tool for making grated butter.

Casserole dishes are used for baking dishes like mashed potatoes, mac and cheese, and layered dishes. They can be made of glass, ceramic, or cast iron. The recipes in this book generally use a 3-quart dish. (For some recipes, you can use a sheet pan in place of a casserole dish.)

A **cast-iron skillet** is a staple tool for Southern cooking and is used for cooking just about everything from desserts to main dishes. These tend to be pricier than nonstick skillets, but they are worth the extra investment; they are sturdier and can withstand high temperatures, which makes them good for deep-frying, as well as other tasks. You can also transfer them from the stovetop to the oven, which is crucial for some soul food recipes.

An **electric hand or stand mixer** will quickly blend ingredients instead of having to mix them by hand.

A **food processor** works the best for puréeing soups and finely grating or chopping ingredients.

Measuring cups and spoons, including large liquid measuring cups for broth and sauces and small measuring spoons for spices and condiments, are needed for many recipes.

Sheet pans are used for roasting and can also be used in place of a casserole dish in some recipes, if needed. The 10-by-15 or 12-by-17 sizes work well.

A **vegetable peeler** is used for peeling potatoes and vegetables.

Whisks are critical for making batters, beating eggs, and whipping cream.

VEGETARIAN SWAPS

Although there are a growing number of fake meats and other kinds of meat substitutes on the market, I generally prefer to swap meat for vegetables or legumes in my recipes. The recipes in this book are made with fresh vegetables, legumes, and other natural substitutes, which are generally more cost-effective (and often healthier). Below I've broken down a few easy swaps that you can refer to quickly to help make any soul food recipe vegetarian.

INSTEAD OF . . .	TRY . . .
Grilled chicken	Portobello mushrooms
Chicken chunks	Cauliflower florets Cubed tofu
Shredded pork, chicken, or beef	Jackfruit
Ground beef	Diced mushrooms, tofu, or cauliflower
Burgers	Black beans, grilled eggplant, or large portobello mushroom
Steak	Cauliflower steak
Sliced steak	Sliced grilled eggplant or portobello mushroom
Bacon slices	Sliced and marinated tempeh
Bacon bits	Marinated tempeh bits or coconut flakes

An **air fryer** fries items quickly without the use of extra oil.

A **citrus squeezer** is a handheld device that can quickly and easily juice citrus on the spot.

A **crock pot** is great to use if you want to slow cook items. They are available in different sizes and are good to use for soups, chili, and rice dishes.

A **mandoline** cuts potatoes, tomatoes, or vegetables into super-thin slices.

Pressure cooker brands like Instant Pot, for example, will help make soups, rice dishes, and beans more quickly.

Salad spinners get leafy greens cleaner and dry faster than you would by hand washing.

Silicone spatulas are helpful when making sauces or batter; they scrape up extra bits of sauce or liquid that normal spoons cannot access.

A **stick (or immersion) blender** is a tall, skinny blender put into large pots to blend soup or sauces. They mean you don't have to move the ingredients back and forth between the pot and a food processor or blender.

A **waffle iron** is the best way to make perfectly formed waffles like my Honey Corn Bread Waffle (page 21). And what goes better with Fried Mushroom "Chicken" (page 74) than that?

ABOUT THE RECIPES

Although soul food is traditionally not about saving time, in the hustle and bustle of today's modern world, people are looking for quicker and easier recipes (see Cooking from Scratch and Shortcuts, page 7). I have developed these recipes with busy people in mind and have included time-saving tips as well. In addition to these tips, you'll find the following labels to indicate when a recipe conforms to other dietary restrictions beyond vegetarianism, or can be made using a very simple cooking method:

- Dairy-free

- Gluten-free

- Nut-free

- Soy-free

- Vegan

- 5-Ingredient (not including oil, water, salt, pepper, or cooking spray)

- One-pot or One-pan (only one cooking vessel needed)

- Under 30 (done in under 30 minutes from start to finish)

Please note that some ingredients, including Parmesan cheese and Worcestershire sauce, may not be vegetarian depending on the brand you use. Always check labels to make sure you are buying a vegetarian-safe product.

Now that you know a bit about the origins and traditions of soul food, you've learned about some of the key vegetarian swaps, and your kitchen is prepared to make soul food vegetarian-style, it's time to get started!

BREAKFAST

◀ *HONEY CORN BREAD WAFFLE, 21*

CREAMY STONE-GROUND GRITS

Serves 4

Prep time: 5 minutes / **Cook time:** 25 minutes

GLUTEN-FREE, NUT-FREE, SOY-FREE, 5-INGREDIENT, ONE-POT, UNDER 30

Grits have been a well-known staple in Southern cooking for centuries. Traditionally served for breakfast, you can now find savory grits all over restaurant menus for dinner. But here we go back to my roots with a traditional grits breakfast: warm, creamy, comforting, and perfect for any day of the week.

1 cup water

2 cups heavy whipping cream

3 tablespoons salted butter, optional

1 teaspoon kosher salt

1 teaspoon ground black pepper

½ cup stone-ground grits (confirm gluten-free if needed)

½ cup shredded Cheddar cheese

1. In a 4-quart pot, combine the water, heavy whipping cream, butter (if using), salt (use more or less to taste), and pepper, and bring it to a boil.

2. Whisk in the grits. Allow the mixture to come back to a low boil, whisking constantly for 5 minutes. After 5 minutes, reduce the heat to low, and cover. Allow it to simmer on low for 20 minutes, whisking occasionally.

3. Remove from the heat, and stir in the shredded cheese. Serve and enjoy.

SUBSTITUTION TIP: For a dairy-free (and vegan) alternative, replace the heavy whipping cream with water, eliminate the butter, and replace the cheese with nutritional yeast.

PREP TIP: If the grits become too thick for your liking, gradually add more heavy whipping cream until they thin out and become smooth and creamy.

GRANDMA'S BISCUITS

Serves 6

Prep time: 15 minutes / **Cook time:** 10 minutes

NUT-FREE, SOY-FREE, 5-INGREDIENT, ONE-PAN, UNDER 30

This classic, warm, flaky biscuit is the perfect addition to any breakfast just about any day of the week, and is complemented by any assortment of toppings.

2 cups self-rising flour, plus more for surface

1½ cups heavy whipping cream

1 teaspoon garlic powder

½ teaspoon kosher salt

2 tablespoons unsalted butter, melted, for brushing

1. Preheat the oven to 500°F. Line a baking sheet with parchment paper.

2. In a mixing bowl, combine the flour, heavy whipping cream, garlic powder, and salt. Mix thoroughly, and knead with your hands until the dough is smooth.

3. Place the dough on a floured surface. Flatten the dough, and use a biscuit cutter to cut out biscuits.

4. Place the biscuits on the prepared baking sheet. Brush each with melted butter. Bake for 10 minutes or until golden brown. Remove from the oven and brush with additional butter if desired. Serve while warm.

RECIPE TIP: These biscuits are best served with the Sawmill Gravy (see page 102). Or, mix it up and try pairing with the Tangy Tomato Gravy (see page 103).

FRIED POTATO AND ONION MEDLEY

Serves 4

Prep time: 5 minutes / **Cook time:** 20 minutes

GLUTEN-FREE, NUT-FREE, SOY-FREE, ONE-PAN, UNDER 30

Crispy yet tender, these melt-in-your-mouth potatoes are the perfect addition to any breakfast. This recipe has been passed down through generations, from my grandmother to my mother and finally down to my sisters and me. The best part of this dish is that it can be served not only for breakfast, but also for lunch or dinner to rave reviews.

2 tablespoons canola oil

2 tablespoons unsalted butter

5 large russet potatoes, chopped into 2-inch chunks

1 large yellow onion, chopped into chunks

1 tablespoon minced garlic

1 teaspoon kosher salt

1 teaspoon ground black pepper

1 teaspoon dried oregano

1 teaspoon paprika

1. In a large skillet, heat the oil and butter over medium-high heat. When hot, add the potatoes, onion, garlic, salt, pepper, oregano, and paprika. Mix thoroughly until all the potatoes and onions are coated with oil and seasonings. Cover, and allow to cook for 10 minutes over medium-low heat, stirring occasionally.

2. After 10 minutes, remove the lid, and continue to cook for an additional 10 minutes, until the potatoes are fork tender. Stir occasionally to ensure that the potatoes do not stick to the bottom of the skillet. Remove from the heat, and serve immediately.

INGREDIENT TIP: Idaho or russet potatoes work best for this recipe. These are the best choice when frying because they are starchy and will hold their shape throughout the frying process.

HONEY CORN BREAD WAFFLE

Serves 4

Prep time: 5 minutes / **Cook time:** 2 to 3 minutes per waffle

NUT-FREE, SOY-FREE, ONE-PAN, UNDER 30

This sweet yet savory honey corn bread waffle is light, fluffy, and sure to become a favorite in your home. The waffle is made using yellow cornmeal, a soul food staple across the South used to prepare hundreds of recipes, including corn bread, Hush Puppies (page 99), Johnny Cakes (page 26), and Corn Bread Dressing (page 96). These waffles are best when topped with either a drizzle of honey or maple syrup and a variety of fruit, or Sawmill Gravy (page 102) for a more savory rendition.

1 cup yellow cornmeal

1 cup all-purpose flour

½ cup granulated white sugar

1 tablespoon ground cinnamon

1 teaspoon baking powder

½ teaspoon baking soda

8 tablespoons (1 stick) unsalted butter, melted

1 cup buttermilk

¼ cup plus 2 tablespoons honey

2 large eggs, beaten

Cooking spray

1. Preheat the waffle iron.

2. In a large mixing bowl, combine the cornmeal, flour, sugar, cinnamon, baking powder, and baking soda. In a separate mixing bowl, combine the melted butter, buttermilk, honey, and beaten eggs. Whisk the ingredients in each bowl thoroughly.

3. Form a well in the middle of the dry mixture. Pour the wet mixture into the well, and gently mix until all ingredients are thoroughly blended.

4. Spray the waffle iron with cooking spray. Pour the waffle batter into the greased waffle iron, and cook for 2 to 3 minutes, depending on your specific waffle iron's instructions. Remove the waffle, and repeat until all the batter is gone. Serve immediately.

LOADED TOMATO OMELET

Serves 2

Prep time: 5 minutes / **Cook time:** 10 minutes

GLUTEN-FREE, NUT-FREE, SOY-FREE, 5-INGREDIENT, ONE-PAN, UNDER 30

The best way to enjoy this cheesy soul food favorite is with fresh ingredients you can enjoy straight from your garden. With freshly plucked tomatoes and eggs from our chickens, this recipe happens to be one of the more whole-some dishes I prepare. Even without your own garden or chickens, though, omelets are a simple and easy breakfast meal, and loading them with fresh vegetables makes them even better. Try adding some green peppers and onions to the mix.

4 large eggs, beaten

½ teaspoon kosher salt

½ teaspoon ground black pepper

2 tablespoons unsalted butter, divided

1 large beefsteak tomato, diced, divided

¼ cup shredded Cheddar cheese, divided

1 tablespoon chopped fresh basil, divided

1. In a medium bowl, whisk together the eggs, salt, and pepper. Set aside.

2. In a small skillet, melt 1 tablespoon of the butter over medium heat. Pour half of the egg mixture into the skillet. Allow it to sit untouched until the edges begin to set, 2 to 3 minutes. With a spatula, lift the edges to allow the uncooked egg to drip into the bottom of the skillet.

3. When the eggs are fully set in the center, place half of the tomatoes, cheese, and basil in the center of the omelet. Fold over and cook for 1 to 2 minutes, until the cheese is melted.

4. Remove from the skillet, repeat for the second omelet, and serve warm.

PREP TIP: Be sure not to overstuff the omelet or it may break apart, causing the filling to fall out.

HASH BROWN CASSEROLE

Serves 8

Prep time: 10 minutes, plus 15 minutes to cool / **Cook time:** 45 minutes

GLUTEN-FREE, NUT-FREE, SOY-FREE, ONE-PAN

There's nothing like this Southern-inspired comfort food. For years my mother and grandmothers have prepared this dish for all kinds of occasions. This creamy, cheesy casserole works well for breakfast or brunch, and its simplicity and affordability make it excellent for huge family gatherings.

4 large russet potatoes, shredded, or 2 pounds frozen (and thawed) hash browns

3 cups shredded Cheddar cheese, divided

1 cup diced yellow onion

2 cups light sour cream

⅔ cup low-fat milk

½ cup (1 stick) unsalted butter, melted

2 tablespoons minced fresh garlic

1 tablespoon dried oregano

1 teaspoon vegetable bouillon (in paste form)

1 teaspoon kosher salt

1 teaspoon ground black pepper

Cooking spray

1. Preheat the oven to 375°F.

2. Drain all excess liquid from the shredded potatoes. Set them aside in a large bowl.

3. In a medium bowl, mix together 2 cups of the cheese, the onion, sour cream, milk, melted butter, garlic, oregano, vegetable base, salt, and pepper. Pour the mixture over the shredded potatoes, and mix until well incorporated.

4. Grease a 9-by-13-inch casserole dish with nonstick cooking spray. Pour the potato mixture into the baking dish, and top with the remaining cheese. Bake for 45 minutes, or until golden brown. Remove from the oven, and allow to cool for at least 15 minutes before serving.

SWEET POTATO FRENCH TOAST CASSEROLE

Serves 6

Prep time: 10 minutes / **Cook time:** 45 minutes

SOY-FREE, ONE-PAN

What better way to enjoy French toast than to sweeten it up a little more? Plus, you're adding superfood sweet potatoes for an infusion of antioxidants and vitamin A. Sweet potatoes are a frequent ingredient in soul food menus. Enslaved Africans traditionally used yams in a lot of their cooking, so sweet potatoes, more commonly grown in the South but quite similar to yams, made their way into many enslaved chefs' desserts and side dishes.

FOR THE CASSEROLE:

Cooking spray

8 large eggs, beaten

2½ cups heavy whipping cream

2 cups cooked, mashed sweet potatoes (see Potato Cakes for mashed potato instructions, page 30)

3 tablespoons granulated white sugar

1 teaspoon ground cinnamon

¼ teaspoon ground nutmeg

1 loaf brioche bread, sliced into 1-inch cubes

FOR THE TOPPING, OPTIONAL:

1 cup unpacked light brown sugar

1 cup chopped pecans

⅓ cup all-purpose flour

4 tablespoons (½ stick) unsalted butter, melted

1 teaspoon ground cinnamon

1 teaspoon ground nutmeg

1. **TO MAKE THE CASSEROLE:** Preheat the oven to 350°F. Spray cooking spray on a 9-by-9-inch casserole dish.

2. In a large mixing bowl, combine the eggs, heavy whipping cream, mashed sweet potatoes, sugar, cinnamon, and nutmeg, and whisk together. Add the bread cubes into the wet mixture, toss until the liquid absorbs into the bread, and set aside.

3. **TO MAKE THE OPTIONAL TOPPING:** In a small mixing bowl, combine the brown sugar, pecans, flour, melted butter, cinnamon, and nutmeg, and whisk well.

4. Pour the French toast cubes into the prepared dish. Sprinkle the topping over the bread mixture. Bake for about 45 minutes, or until the top is golden brown.

SUBSTITUTION TIP: If you opt out of the pecan topping, consider serving this casserole topped with honey, maple syrup, fresh fruit, or compote.

JOHNNY CAKES

Serves 4

Prep time: 5 minutes / **Cook time:** 6 minutes per batch

NUT-FREE, SOY-FREE, ONE-PAN, UNDER 30

Johnny Cakes, also known as hoecakes (because of how enslaved people cooked them on the blade of a hoe) and journey cakes (because they were easy to carry and prepare on long journeys), have been around for centuries. Originating with Native Americans and adopted by enslaved people, they are basically delicious cornmeal flatbreads that resemble pancakes. Enjoy these with some drizzled honey.

1 tablespoon vegetable oil

1 large egg, beaten

1 cup buttermilk

1 cup all-purpose flour

½ cup cornmeal

1 tablespoon baking powder

2 tablespoons granulated white sugar

½ teaspoon kosher salt

1 tablespoon unsalted butter

Honey, for serving, optional

1. In a medium mixing bowl, combine the oil, egg, and buttermilk, and whisk together. In a separate large mixing bowl, combine the flour, cornmeal, baking powder, sugar, and salt, and mix together. Pour the wet ingredients into the bowl with the dry ingredients, and mix well.

2. In a large skillet, melt the butter over medium-low heat. Add about ¼-cup dollops of batter into the greased skillet, leaving 1 inch between each dollop. You will need to do this in 2 batches.

3. Cook over medium-low heat for about 3 minutes per side. Flip when the tops are bubbling. When golden brown, remove the cakes from the skillet, and serve drizzled with honey (if using).

SWEET POTATO HASH

Serves 4

Prep time: 10 minutes, plus 5 minutes to cool / **Cook time:** 45 minutes

DAIRY-FREE, GLUTEN-FREE, NUT-FREE, SOY-FREE, VEGAN, ONE-PAN

This is an ideal vegetarian take on an age-old Southern classic: hash. Usually made with pork and white potatoes, this heathy, fresh version derives its fiber from sweet potatoes, its healthy fat from olive oil, and its vitamins and minerals from the fresh veggies and herbs. Though it's no less filling or delicious than the traditional version, it's far more nutritious.

Cooking spray

4 large sweet potatoes, peeled and cut into 1½-inch chunks

1 large yellow onion, chopped into chunks

1 large red bell pepper, diced

3 tablespoons olive oil

2 tablespoons minced fresh garlic

1 tablespoon dried oregano

1 teaspoon dried rosemary

1 teaspoon kosher salt

1 teaspoon ground black pepper

1. Preheat the oven to 400°F. Prepare a baking sheet by spraying it with cooking spray.

2. In a large mixing bowl, combine the sweet potatoes, onion, bell pepper, olive oil, garlic, oregano, rosemary, salt, and pepper (use more or less to taste). Toss thoroughly to coat.

3. Pour the mixture onto the prepared baking sheet, and place it into the oven. Bake for about 45 minutes or until the potatoes are tender. Be sure to rotate the potatoes once halfway through the cooking process to ensure even cooking. Remove from the oven, and set aside to cool for 5 minutes before serving.

SUBSTITUTION TIP: For an added smoky flavor, add ½ tablespoon cayenne pepper and 1 teaspoon smoked paprika.

OLD-FASHIONED CINNAMON APPLE OATMEAL

Serves 4

Prep time: 5 minutes / **Cook time:** 25 minutes

DAIRY-FREE, GLUTEN-FREE, SOY-FREE, 5-INGREDIENT, ONE-POT, UNDER 30

When I was a child, my grandmother would prepare a creamy bowl of oatmeal for my breakfast, and we would watch her "shows." Although I wasn't so fond of her shows, I did love the time together, so this old-fashioned oatmeal recipe brings me back to those special moments, and it is a recipe that I will forever love and cherish.

2 cups water

2 cups almond milk

½ teaspoon kosher salt

2 cups old-fashioned rolled oats

2 cups chopped Granny Smith apples

½ cup unpacked light brown sugar

2 tablespoons honey, for serving, optional

1. In a large pot, combine the water, almond milk, and salt, and bring to a boil over high heat.

2. Add the oats to the pot, and reduce heat to medium-low. Cook for 5 minutes. Add the chopped apples and brown sugar. Allow the oatmeal to simmer for 15 minutes, stirring occasionally, until it is thick and creamy.

3. Remove from the heat, and cover with a lid until ready to serve. Serve with a drizzle of honey, if desired.

PREP TIP: Top the oatmeal with additional fruit, nuts, or raisins to make this dish even heartier.

BUTTERMILK "FLAPJACK" PANCAKES

Serves 4

Prep time: 5 minutes / **Cook time:** 6 minutes per batch

SOY-FREE, ONE-PAN, UNDER 30

Buttermilk pancakes, best known as "flapjacks" in the South, are actually a breakfast staple all over the world in various incarnations. When prepared on a hot griddle or cast-iron skillet, this recipe provides the perfect crispy edges and fluffy interior. Over the past 25 years, my brother-in-law has made it his personal mission to perfect this delicacy. Topping options are endless and completely up to you.

1¼ cups all-purpose flour

1 tablespoon baking powder

1 tablespoon granulated white sugar

½ teaspoon ground cinnamon

¼ teaspoon kosher salt

1 cup buttermilk

4 tablespoons (½ stick) unsalted butter, melted

2 large eggs, beaten

1 teaspoon pure vanilla extract

2 tablespoons coconut oil (or additional melted butter), for the skillet

1. In a medium mixing bowl, combine the flour, baking powder, sugar, cinnamon, and salt. In a separate small mixing bowl, combine the buttermilk, melted butter, beaten eggs, and vanilla. Slowly pour the wet ingredients into the dry ingredients. Whisk thoroughly until the batter is a smooth consistency.

2. In a large skillet, preheat the coconut oil over medium-low heat. Measure ¼-cup dollops of the batter, and place them in the skillet, leaving 1 inch between each dollop. Cook the pancakes for 2 to 3 minutes on the first side, flip them when they start to bubble, and then cook them for 2 to 3 minutes on the reverse side. Work in batches, if necessary. Remove the pancakes from the skillet when they are golden brown, and serve with your toppings of choice.

PREP TIP: Make these pancakes your own. They can be filled with fruits such as blueberries, nuts, and even chocolate chips.

POTATO CAKES

Serves 4

Prep time: 10 minutes / **Cook time:** 15 minutes

NUT-FREE, SOY-FREE, UNDER 30

Growing up, we ate these potato cakes any time we were craving something hearty. They are a quick, easy, and affordable dish packed with flavor. You can even make them using leftover mashed potatoes. Chunky on the outside and creamy on the inside, you too will find these hard to resist, especially when served with Vegan Collard Greens (page 34).

1 cup canola oil

4 large russet potatoes, peeled and cut into 1-inch cubes

1 tablespoon plus 1 teaspoon kosher salt, divided

1 cup shredded Cheddar cheese

½ cup all-purpose flour

4 tablespoons (½ stick) unsalted butter, melted

1 large egg, beaten

1 teaspoon ground black pepper

1 teaspoon dried oregano

1. In a large skillet, preheat the oil over medium heat.

2. Meanwhile, in a large pot, cover the potato cubes with water (about 1 inch above the potatoes). Add 1 tablespoon of salt, and boil for about 8 minutes, or until fork tender. Drain the water from the potatoes and place them in a large bowl. Mash the potatoes with a potato masher until smooth. Set aside.

3. In a medium mixing bowl, combine the cheese, flour, melted butter, egg, the remaining teaspoon of salt, the pepper, and oregano. Mix thoroughly. Pour the mixture into the mashed potatoes and stir to combine.

4. Scoop out the potato mixture using a ½-cup scoop. Pat each cake flat, and place them in the hot oil. Fry them for 3 minutes on each side, until golden brown. Remove from the oil, and drain on paper towels. Serve immediately while warm.

SUBSTITUTION TIP: Bake these potato cakes instead of frying them for heart-healthier version. Bake them on a greased baking sheet for 30 minutes at 375°F. Flip them once in the middle of the cooking time.

CHAPTER 3

SALADS, SIDES, AND APPETIZERS

◀ *SOUTHERN BAKED MAC AND CHEESE, 39*

VEGAN COLLARD GREENS

Serves 6

Prep time: 5 minutes / **Cook time:** 45 minutes

DAIRY-FREE, GLUTEN-FREE, NUT-FREE, SOY-FREE, VEGAN, ONE-POT

Introduced to the South by enslaved individuals, traditional soul food collard greens are seasoned with bacon or ham hock. Here, I offer you a vegetarian version of the age-old Southern favorite without sacrificing any taste at all. Collard greens are an excellent way to add some antioxidants, vitamins, minerals, and soul to any diet. Serve with any Sunday dinner, like Fried Mushroom "Chicken" (page 74) or Southern Baked Mac and Cheese (page 39).

2 tablespoons olive oil

½ cup diced red bell pepper

½ cup diced white onion

2 garlic cloves, finely chopped

3 cups vegetable broth

1 bunch collard greens, cleaned, de-stemmed, and shredded (see Ingredient Tip below)

2 tablespoons apple cider vinegar

1 teaspoon granulated white sugar

1 teaspoon red pepper flakes

1 teaspoon kosher salt

1 teaspoon black pepper

1. In a large pot, combine the olive oil, bell pepper, onion, and garlic. Sauté over medium-low heat for about 5 minutes, or until fragrant. Add the vegetable broth and scrape the bottom of the pot to deglaze.

2. Add the collard greens, vinegar, sugar, red pepper flakes, salt, and pepper, and stir. Cover, and simmer over medium-low for 40 minutes.

3. Remove from the heat, and serve warm.

INGREDIENT TIP: If using pre-shredded and packaged collards, use a 32-ounce bag.

VARIATION TIP: Switch it up by using turnip greens in place of collards. High in nutrients and low in calories, turnip greens have a place in soul food all their own. Traditionally cooked on New Year's Eve along with black-eyed peas, the greens are said to represent money for the new year ahead, while the black-eyed peas are said to bring good luck.

CANDIED YAMS

Serves 6

Prep time: 5 minutes, plus 10 minutes to cool / **Cook time:** 1 hour and 5 minutes

GLUTEN-FREE, NUT-FREE, SOY-FREE

Yams, often confused with sweet potatoes, are smaller and starchier than their larger siblings. Though you might be hard-pressed to find actual yams in the US, this soul food dish retains the name. The sweet homemade glaze propels this dish to perfection—which explains why this is a must-have Thanksgiving dish when it comes to Southern households. You still get all of the health benefits but in a dish so sweet and so delicious, you may confuse it with dessert.

Cooking spray

6 large sweet potatoes, peeled and quartered

1 cup unpacked light brown sugar

½ cup unsalted butter, melted

½ cup pure maple syrup

¼ cup granulated white sugar

1 tablespoon ground cinnamon

1 teaspoon pure vanilla extract

¼ teaspoon ground nutmeg

¼ teaspoon ground ginger

1. Preheat the oven to 350°F. Grease a 9-by-13-inch baking dish with cooking spray. Put the sweet potato pieces into the baking dish and set aside.

2. In a medium saucepan, combine the brown sugar, melted butter, maple syrup, granulated sugar, cinnamon, vanilla, nutmeg, and ginger. Mix thoroughly over medium-low heat. Allow the sauce to simmer for 2 to 3 minutes, then remove from the heat.

3. Pour the sauce over the sweet potatoes and stir to fully coat. Cover the dish loosely with aluminum foil, and bake for 40 minutes, stirring occasionally.

4. After 40 minutes, remove the foil, and bake for an additional 20 minutes. Remove the dish from the oven, and allow it to cool for 10 minutes before serving.

PREP TIP: If sauce becomes too thin after baking, allow the dish to sit at room temperature for at least 30 minutes. The sauce will thicken on its own.

SUCCOTASH

Serves 6

Prep time: 15 minutes / **Cook time:** 25 minutes

GLUTEN-FREE, NUT-FREE, SOY-FREE, ONE-POT

Succotash is a delicious side dish known for its sweet corn and lima bean combination. With its long history dating back to the 17th century, it is traditionally prepared along with a Thanksgiving meal. This recipe has evolved over the years from a simple bean-and-corn mixture to being substantially veggie-packed and full of flavor.

1 tablespoon olive oil
1 yellow onion, diced
2 garlic cloves, minced
2 cups frozen lima beans, thawed

8 fresh ears of corn (or 4 cups of frozen corn), kernels sliced off
3 tablespoons salted butter
1 small tomato, diced

½ teaspoon cayenne pepper
1 pinch of sugar, optional
Kosher salt
Ground black pepper

1. Heat the olive oil in a large skillet. Add the onion and garlic, and sauté over medium heat for 1 to 2 minutes until the garlic is fragrant.

2. Stir in the lima beans, corn kernels, and butter. Allow to cook for 15 minutes, stirring frequently.

3. Stir in the tomato, cayenne pepper, sugar (if using), salt, and pepper. Taste and adjust seasoning as necessary.

4. Allow to cook for an additional 5 minutes, then remove from heat.

5. Serve while warm.

PREP TIP: Cut corn kernels off the cob by placing a cob upright in a large bowl and cutting downward—this prevents the kernels from flying away.

DEVILED EGGS

Serves 8

Prep time: 10 minutes / **Cook time:** 15 minutes

GLUTEN-FREE, NUT-FREE, ONE-POT, UNDER 30

The term "deviled" here originated due to the spicy flavors incorporated into the recipe dating back to the 18th century. But rather than focusing on spice, this filling uses a combination of cool and refreshing condiments. These classic bites are a great treat for anything from a casual dinner to special occasions such as baby showers!

8 large eggs

1 tablespoon baking soda

¼ cup Miracle Whip dressing

2 teaspoons yellow mustard

2 teaspoons sweet relish

Kosher salt

Ground black pepper

1 tablespoon paprika, for garnish

1 tablespoon parsley, for garnish

1. Add the whole eggs to a large pot and cover with water. Add baking soda (which helps the shells be easily removed later on), and bring to a boil. Boil the eggs for about 12 to 14 minutes. Drain and place directly into cold water to chill and stop the cooking process.

2. Once chilled, carefully remove the shells from the eggs and discard. Slice each egg in half lengthwise.

3. Remove the yolks and spoon them into a bowl. Mash them with a fork until the yolks are in fine pieces.

4. Add the Miracle Whip, mustard, relish, salt, and pepper and mix until smooth. Adjust seasonings to taste. Use a small spoon to carefully divide the filling between the egg halves (or use a piping bag if you want them to look a little fancier).

5. Sprinkle paprika and parsley on the eggs. Enjoy!

RECIPE TIP: Deviled eggs are best served cold. Refrigerate for at least 2 hours if you can wait to dig in.

COLESLAW FROM SCRATCH

Serves 6
Prep time: 10 minutes

GLUTEN-FREE, NUT-FREE, ONE-POT, UNDER 30

Cabbage has long been a staple of soul food because it was inexpensive, available, filling, and easy to make delicious. Coleslaw, also known as cabbage salad, is a long-standing tradition in the South, practically expected at a barbecue or potluck. My mother has always made her coleslaw from scratch because nothing says flavor like doing it yourself with your own fresh ingredients. Serve it with Chopped Barbecue Sliders (page 88).

1 medium green cabbage, shredded

1 cup finely shredded carrots

2 tablespoons finely diced white onion

Juice of 1 lemon

½ cup light mayonnaise

¼ cup cold buttermilk

1 tablespoon apple cider vinegar

1 teaspoon granulated white sugar, optional

½ teaspoon kosher salt

½ teaspoon black pepper

1. In a medium mixing bowl, combine the cabbage, carrots, and onion.

2. In a separate small mixing bowl, whisk together the lemon juice, mayonnaise, buttermilk, vinegar, sugar (if using), salt, and pepper until smooth. Pour the wet mixture over the cabbage mixture, and mix together thoroughly.

3. Adjust the seasonings to taste, and refrigerate until ready to serve.

PREP TIP: Coleslaw can be made in advance and refrigerated in an airtight container in the refrigerator for up to one week.

SOUTHERN BAKED MAC AND CHEESE

Serves 8

Prep time: 10 minutes, plus 25 minutes to cool / **Cook time:** 1 hour

NUT-FREE, SOY-FREE, ONE-PAN

This is the quintessential crowd pleaser. There are as many versions as there are people who make it. I felt I had to make my own version, with my own unique cheese blend and spices. Sometimes, you just have to go all out.

Cooking spray

1 pound elbow macaroni noodles

2 tablespoons unsalted butter

1 cup heavy whipping cream

1 cup whole milk

¾ cup light sour cream

3 large eggs, beaten

1½ cups shredded mild Cheddar cheese

½ cup shredded sharp Cheddar cheese

½ cup shredded smoked Gouda cheese

1 teaspoon kosher salt

1 teaspoon ground black pepper

1 cup shredded Colby jack cheese

2 tablespoons chopped fresh parsley

Paprika, for garnish

1. Preheat the oven to 350°F. Grease an 11-inch baking dish with cooking spray (or use your favorite cast iron skillet).

2. Boil the noodles according to package instructions. Drain them and put them in a large bowl. Add butter and stir until it is melted. Set aside.

3. In a medium mixing bowl, combine the cream, milk, sour cream, eggs, both cheddars, Gouda, salt, and pepper. Pour the custard over the cooked pasta and gently stir until well incorporated.

4. Pour the mixture into the greased baking dish. Top with the Colby jack cheese, parsley, and a paprika sprinkle, cover with foil, and bake for 30 minutes.

5. After 30 minutes, remove the foil, and bake for 15 minutes or until golden brown. Remove from the oven, and allow to cool for at least 25 minutes before serving.

SUBSTITUTION TIP: For a lighter version, eliminate the butter, replace the whole milk with almond milk, and replace the Colby jack cheese with cashew cheese.

TRADITIONAL FRIED OKRA

Serves 4

Prep time: 5 minutes / **Cook time:** 10 minutes

DAIRY-FREE, GLUTEN-FREE, NUT-FREE, SOY-FREE,
5-INGREDIENT, ONE-PAN, UNDER 30

Okra was one of the few crops brought over from Africa during the slave trade era. It has turned out to be one of the most delicious and common ingredients used in Southern cooking today. Not only does okra taste good, but it also boasts numerous health benefits like lowering heart disease and blood sugar. Try the Spicy Baked Popcorn "Shrimp" with Okra, page 41, for a less traditional but healthier preparation of okra bites.

2 cups canola oil

10 fresh okra pods, cut in ½-inch slices (see Ingredient Tip below)

1 large egg, beaten, for egg wash

1 cup yellow cornmeal

½ teaspoon kosher salt

½ teaspoon ground black pepper

¼ teaspoon cayenne pepper

1. In a large skillet, preheat the oil over medium heat. In a bowl, soak the okra in the egg wash while the oil is preheating.

2. In a separate medium mixing bowl, combine the cornmeal, salt, black pepper, and cayenne pepper. Remove the okra pieces from the egg wash, and coat them thoroughly in the cornmeal mixture.

3. Place the okra pieces in the heated oil and fry for 8 to 10 minutes, until golden brown.

4. Remove the okra from the oil, place on paper towels to drain the excess oil, and serve.

INGREDIENT TIP: If you do not have fresh okra, feel free to use frozen (and defrosted) chopped okra. Fresh okra is available in grocery stores and, even fresher, at farmers' markets.

SPICY BAKED POPCORN "SHRIMP" WITH OKRA

Serves 6

Prep time: 10 minutes, plus 20 minutes to marinate and freeze / **Cook time:** 25 minutes

NUT-FREE, SOY-FREE, ONE-PAN

This vegetarian version of "popcorn shrimp" is a popular snack in homes across the South. Rather than deep-frying the okra, here I bake it to avoid the extra oil and fat. Double-battering adds that extra crispiness, but you'll really be able to take advantage of the fact that okra is so nutritious, containing vitamins C and K and numerous antioxidants. This popcorn "shrimp" can be served as a filling entrée, if paired with rice.

2 cups whole okra pods, fresh or frozen and thawed

1 cup Italian-style bread crumbs

1 cup buttermilk

1 large egg, beaten

1 tablespoon onion powder

1 tablespoon garlic powder

½ tablespoon cayenne pepper

1 tablespoon hot sauce

1 teaspoon smoked paprika

1 teaspoon kosher salt

Cooking spray

1. Preheat the oven to 325°F. Wash and dry the okra.

2. Put the bread crumbs in a small bowl and set aside. In a medium mixing bowl, thoroughly combine the buttermilk, egg, onion powder, garlic powder, cayenne pepper, hot sauce, paprika, and salt.

3. Place the okra pods in the buttermilk mixture, and allow them to marinate for at least 10 minutes. Remove the okra pods, and toss them into the bread crumbs until fully coated. To double batter, briefly toss them back into the wet mixture, and then into the dry batter once again.

4. Place the fully coated okra onto a plate, and freeze for 10 minutes to ensure the batter stays adhered during baking.

5. Coat a baking sheet with cooking spray and place the okra on it. Bake for about 25 minutes or until golden brown, flipping halfway through. Serve.

BARBECUE BAKED BEANS

Serves 8

Prep time: 5 minutes / **Cook time:** 45 minutes

DAIRY-FREE, GLUTEN-FREE, NUT-FREE, SOY-FREE, ONE-PAN

Simple to make but tangy and delicious to eat, these beans pair with anything coming off the grill, especially corn on the cob. The twist of extra flavors I add makes them a true standout on any potluck table. Adding a touch of liquid smoke enhances the flavor by giving the beans that authentic smoky finish.

3 (15-ounce) cans vegetarian baked beans, drained

¾ cup barbecue sauce

½ cup fresh pineapple juice

½ cup unpacked light brown sugar

½ green bell pepper, diced

½ yellow onion, diced

2 tablespoons yellow mustard

1 teaspoon onion powder

1 teaspoon garlic powder

½ teaspoon liquid smoke

1. Preheat the oven to 375°F.

2. In a 9-by-13-inch baking dish, combine the beans, barbecue sauce, pineapple juice, brown sugar, bell pepper, onion, mustard, onion powder, garlic powder, and liquid smoke, and mix thoroughly.

3. Place the baking dish in the oven, and bake for 45 minutes. Remove from the oven, and enjoy immediately.

PREP TIP: If you would like to cook this dish on the grill, omit the liquid smoke and cook for 45 minutes in a 15-inch cast-iron skillet. The natural smoke from the grill will provide that smoky flavor.

RECIPE TIP: For a quick and easy homemade barbecue sauce, in a small saucepan over medium heat, whisk together 1 cup ketchup; ¼ cup dark brown sugar; 1 tablespoon each of apple cider vinegar, honey, and coconut aminos; and 1 teaspoon each of liquid smoke, garlic powder, and cayenne pepper. Allow to simmer for 8 minutes until thick; taste to adjust seasonings, then remove from the heat and serve when cool.

LUCKY BLACK-EYED PEAS

Serves 6

Prep time: 5 minutes / **Cook time:** 1 hour and 5 minutes

DAIRY-FREE, GLUTEN-FREE, NUT-FREE, SOY-FREE, VEGAN,
5-INGREDIENT, ONE-POT

Black-eyed peas have been a traditional side dish among African American families for centuries. It's common to cook black-eyed peas on New Year's Eve to bring good luck for the year to come. This tradition continues in many families today. They pair beautifully with Fried Green Tomatoes (page 48).

2 tablespoons olive oil

1 cup finely diced white onion

2 garlic cloves, minced

8 cups vegetable broth

1 (16-ounce) bag dried or frozen black-eyed peas

1 teaspoon kosher salt

1 teaspoon black pepper

1 teaspoon red pepper flakes

1. In a large pot, sauté the olive oil, onion, and garlic over medium heat. Allow to cook for 4 to 5 minutes, until fragrant. Add in the vegetable broth and black-eyed peas, and stir thoroughly. Cover and simmer on medium-low heat for about 1 hour.

2. Remove from the heat, and add the salt, pepper, and red pepper flakes (adjust amounts to taste) before enjoying.

SAUTÉED SEASONED CABBAGE

Serves 6

Prep time: 5 minutes / **Cook time:** 15 minutes

GLUTEN-FREE, NUT-FREE, SOY-FREE, 5-INGREDIENT, ONE-PAN, UNDER 30

This recipe is a twist on the traditional fried cabbage so popular in soul food. Cabbage is one of the most versatile vegetables. It can be fried, steamed, sautéed, or even baked and still turn out delicious all the same. The traditional version of this dish has bacon frying with the cabbage. My version skips the bacon, but with just a few vegetarian-friendly ingredients, this recipe still provides the warmth and comfort of any soul food dish. For a vegan version, use 2 tablespoons of olive oil instead of the butter.

4 tablespoons (½ stick) salted butter

½ white onion, diced

1 large head green cabbage, chopped into chunks

1 teaspoon Creole seasoning

1 teaspoon ground black pepper

1 teaspoon granulated white sugar

½ teaspoon kosher salt, optional

1. In a large skillet, heat the butter and onion over medium heat. Cook for 3 to 4 minutes, until translucent.

2. Add the cabbage, Creole seasoning, pepper, sugar, and salt (if using), and stir. Cover with a lid, raise the heat to medium-high, and allow the cabbage to cook for 10 minutes, stirring occasionally.

3. Remove from the heat, and enjoy.

PREP TIP: For faster cooking, slice your cabbage into thin strips instead of chunks.

CORN PUDDIN'

Serves 6

Prep time: 5 minutes / **Cook time:** 1 hour

GLUTEN-FREE, NUT-FREE, SOY-FREE

Comfort. That's what comes to mind when making and enjoying this dish. It brings back memories of having Sunday dinner at grandma's, family around the table, and corn puddin' at the center of attention. Whether you call it corn puddin' or corn casserole, this dish is sure to become a family favorite in your home, just as it is in ours. And to enhance this indulgence even more, my version has a little extra sugar and cinnamon.

8 tablespoons (1 stick) unsalted butter

2½ cups frozen corn, defrosted

1 (16-ounce) can cream-style corn

¾ cup heavy whipping cream

2 large eggs, beaten

½ cup yellow cornmeal

⅓ cup granulated white sugar

¼ cup whole milk

½ tablespoon ground cinnamon

1 teaspoon kosher salt

1. Preheat the oven to 375°F.

2. In a 9-by-13-inch casserole dish, melt the butter in the preheated oven for about 3 minutes. Remove it from the oven, and grease the pan with the butter. Set it aside.

3. In a large mixing bowl, combine the frozen corn, cream-style corn, whipping cream, eggs, cornmeal, sugar, milk, cinnamon, and salt. Pour the mixture into the buttered baking dish, and mix together until the butter is thoroughly combined into the mixture.

4. Place it back in the oven, and bake for 1 hour or until golden brown. Remove it from the oven, and enjoy.

CREAMY POTATO SALAD

Serves 6

Prep time: 20 minutes, plus 2½ to 3½ hours to cool / **Cook time:** 10 minutes

DAIRY-FREE, NUT-FREE, ONE-POT

Potato salad is a side dish you'll find at practically every Southern family function, Sunday dinner, and holiday celebration. Many different cultures and types of cuisine call it their own, each with their own spin on it. In recent years, people have branched out to experiment with different ingredients in their potato salads, adding things like hummus, nuts, grapes, and even raisins. This recipe sticks closely to tradition, featuring ingredients that are bound to remind you of how it has been made for over 100 years.

5 Yukon Gold potatoes, peeled and diced

3 tablespoons kosher salt, divided

5 hard-boiled eggs, peeled and diced (see Prep Tip below)

2 cups light mayonnaise

½ cup sweet salad cubes (chunky-cut sweet pickles)

¼ cup yellow mustard

1 tablespoon garlic powder

1 tablespoon onion powder

1 tablespoon granulated white sugar

½ tablespoon ground black pepper

Ground paprika, for garnish

1. In a large pot, cover the diced potatoes with water by at least 1 inch, add 2 tablespoons of salt, and stir. Bring the potatoes to a boil over high heat, then maintain a boil for 8 to 10 minutes, or until they are fork tender. Remove from the heat, and drain the water from the potatoes. Put the drained potatoes into a large bowl, and refrigerate them for 25 minutes or until cool.

2. While the potatoes chill, in a medium mixing bowl combine the remaining 1 tablespoon salt, the eggs, mayonnaise, sweet salad cubes, mustard, garlic powder, onion powder, sugar, and pepper. When the mixture is well combined, taste and adjust seasonings based on preference.

3. Remove the potatoes from the refrigerator. Pour the wet mixture onto the cooked and cooled potatoes, and stir gently. Be sure not to overmix, or the potatoes will become too soft and mushy, more like mashed potatoes.

4. Garnish with paprika, refrigerate 2 to 3 hours until cold, and serve.

INGREDIENT TIP: If using Miracle Whip instead of mayonnaise, feel free to omit the sugar, because Miracle Whip contains enough sweetness.

PREP TIP: To hard boil eggs, place eggs in a pot, and add water to cover the eggs completely. Bring it to a boil, and let them boil for 12 minutes. Cool in an ice bath before peeling and dicing.

FRIED GREEN TOMATOES

Serves 4

Prep time: 5 minutes / **Cook time:** 8 minutes per batch

NUT-FREE, SOY-FREE, ONE-PAN, UNDER 30

This quintessential Southern dish did not actually originate in the South, but rather is rumored to have been brought over by European Jewish immigrants to the North and Midwest. Nonetheless, Southern cuisine has made this dish its very own, enjoying fried green tomatoes for generations, and even claiming a book (and movie) about them. With your favorite dipping sauce like ranch or blue cheese, there is no more Southern, or irresistible, snack. Try serving them with Cabbage Soup with Veggies (page 54) for an unbelievable match.

2 cups canola oil

4 large green tomatoes

1 cup all-purpose flour

1 teaspoon kosher salt

1 teaspoon ground black pepper

1 teaspoon paprika

2 large eggs, beaten

½ cup whole milk

¾ cup cornmeal

½ cup bread crumbs

1 tablespoon garlic powder

1. In a large skillet, preheat the oil over medium heat.

2. Slice the tomatoes into ½-inch-thick slices, and set them aside on paper towels.

3. In a small mixing bowl, combine the flour, salt, pepper, and paprika. Mix well. In a separate small mixing bowl, whisk together the eggs and milk. In a third small mixing bowl, combine the cornmeal, bread crumbs, and garlic powder.

4. Dredge each tomato slice in the flour mixture, then the egg mixture, and finally the cornmeal mixture. Ensure that they are fully coated.

5. Place the fully coated tomatoes in the hot oil, and fry for about 4 minutes on each side or until golden brown. Work in batches if you need to.

6. Remove the tomatoes from the oil, and set them aside on paper towels to drain. Enjoy them with your favorite dipping sauce.

SUBSTITUTION TIP: For additional flavor, feel free to use seasoned bread crumbs instead of plain.

SAUTÉED GREEN BEANS

Serves 4

Prep time: 5 minutes / **Cook time:** 8 minutes

GLUTEN-FREE, NUT-FREE, SOY-FREE, 5-INGREDIENT, ONE-PAN, UNDER 30

Green beans have long been popular soul food sides, traditionally boiled and cooked with broth and ham hock. Add some nutrients along with some fresh flavor with this simple version of the side dish. A great source of fiber, vitamin K, and calcium, green beans are a healthy crunchy bite, perfect for any dinner table spread. Serve them with mashed potatoes and Mushroom Gravy Smothered Burgers (page 82).

1 tablespoon olive oil

1 garlic clove, minced

1 tablespoon salted butter

4 cups fresh green beans

1 teaspoon ground black pepper

1 teaspoon sea salt, optional

1. In a medium skillet, combine the olive oil, garlic, and butter. Set the burner to medium heat, and stir continuously for 1 minute or until fragrant.

2. Add the green beans to the skillet. Add pepper and salt (if using), and stir to coat the green beans. Cook for 7 minutes, continuously stirring the green beans to ensure that they do not burn. Remove from the heat, and enjoy.

SUBSTITUTION TIP: Fresh green beans can be replaced with 4 cups of frozen green beans for the same fresh taste with the perfect crunch in every bite. Also, if you eliminate the butter, this recipe becomes vegan and dairy-free.

CORN FRITTER TREAT

Serves 4

Prep time: 5 minutes / **Cook time:** 8 minutes

Corn fritters have been around for generations, and will be around for generations to come. And it's easy to see why; they are the perfect between-meal treat. With the creamy sweet corn on the inside and the crunchy crust, they are truly hard to resist. The touch of sugar really enhances all of the flavors. See the Substitution Tip below for a baked version.

2 cups canola oil

1 cup fresh sweet corn or frozen corn, defrosted

1 cup self-rising flour

1 large egg, beaten

½ cup whole milk

¼ cup granulated white sugar

1 teaspoon kosher salt

2 teaspoons honey, warmed for serving, optional

1. In a large skillet, preheat the oil over medium heat.

2. Meanwhile, in a medium mixing bowl, combine the corn, flour, egg, milk, sugar, and salt. Mix well. Form ¼ cup of the fritter mixture into a small patty, and place it in the hot oil. Repeat this until you have 4 fritters in your skillet.

3. Cook the fritters for about 4 minutes on each side, or until golden brown. Remove the fritters from the oil, and drain on paper towels. Enjoy while warm. Drizzle with honey (if using) for extra sweetness.

SUBSTITUTION TIP: For a healthier twist on fritters, try baking them. Add ½ teaspoon of baking powder to the mix, pour the batter into a greased muffin pan, and bake at 400°F for 15 minutes or until golden brown.

PASTA SALAD

Serves 8

Prep time: 15 minutes, plus at least 2 hours to chill / **Cook time:** 8 minutes

NUT-FREE, ONE-POT

This chilled and fragrant dish is easily identified by its colorful appearance. Pasta salad can be a delicious main dish, side, or appetizer, but any way it's served, you can't forget the delicious blend of veggies, dressing, and pasta. This is often regarded as a spring or summertime meal, but after trying this recipe, you'll crave it year-round. I like to make this for summer barbecues and it pairs well alongside our Barbecue Baked Beans (page 42).

1 pound tri-color rotini pasta

1 (24-ounce) bottle Italian dressing

3 cups cherry tomatoes, halved

½ cup diced green bell pepper

½ cup diced cucumber

½ cup shredded carrot

½ cup diced red onion

1 teaspoon salt

1 teaspoon pepper

½ cup shredded Cheddar cheese

1. Boil the pasta according to the package instructions. Drain the pasta and transfer to a large mixing bowl to cool.

2. Once cooled, add the dressing, tomatoes, bell pepper, cucumber, carrot, onion, salt, and pepper into the bowl and mix together with the pasta. After it is mixed thoroughly, taste and adjust seasonings if needed.

3. Sprinkle the shredded cheese on top.

4. Refrigerate for at least 2 hours, or even overnight for the best flavor.

VARIATION TIP: Feel free to use additional toppings such as black olives along with the shredded cheese.

CHAPTER 4

SOUPS AND STEWS

◄ BLACK-EYED PEA SOUP, 64

CABBAGE SOUP WITH VEGGIES

Serves 4 to 6

Prep time: 10 minutes / **Cook time:** 30 minutes

DAIRY-FREE, GLUTEN-FREE, NUT-FREE, SOY-FREE, VEGAN, ONE-POT

Growing up, during the winter months, this cabbage soup happened to be one of my favorite soups, which was lucky because it's such a healthy one. My sister and I used to spend time helping my mother prepare this dish by cleaning and chopping the cabbage right alongside her, learning everything step by step. One of the best parts about preparing this dish is that it can be frozen and stored for up to 6 months until you are ready to enjoy it again.

4 tablespoons olive oil

2 large carrots, chopped

¾ cup chopped celery

¾ cup diced white onion

4 garlic cloves, minced

1 head green cabbage, shredded

4 large beefsteak tomatoes, diced

8 cups vegetable broth

1½ cups tomato juice

1 teaspoon dried thyme

Kosher salt

Ground black pepper

1. In a large pot, heat the oil over medium heat. Add the carrots, celery, and onion to the oil, stir, and allow to cook for 5 minutes. Add in the garlic, and stir for an additional 1 minute.

2. Add the cabbage and tomatoes. Stir and allow them to cook for 4 to 5 minutes. Add the broth, tomato juice, thyme, and salt and pepper to taste. Allow the soup to simmer over medium heat for at least 20 minutes. Serve warm.

INGREDIENT TIP: For your convenience, this recipe also works well with 1 (15-ounce) can of stewed tomatoes.

SWEET STEWED CORN

Serves 4

Prep time: 10 minutes / **Cook time:** 20 minutes

GLUTEN-FREE, NUT-FREE, SOY-FREE, 5-INGREDIENT, ONE-POT, UNDER 30

Stewed corn, fried corn, corn pudding, corn casserole—the list goes on. Corn is such a widely available, inexpensive, and versatile food, it's no wonder there are so many variants of it in traditional (and current) soul food. This stewed corn is a true soul food gem. Traditionally prepared with bacon drippings, this version yields as much flavor without it, because fresh sweet corn is the star. And as my grandmother would say, the sweeter the better.

6 ears white corn

4 tablespoons (½ stick) salted butter

2 tablespoons olive oil

1 teaspoon granulated white sugar, optional

Kosher salt

Ground black pepper

1. Cut the corn kernels from the cobs using a sharp knife (see the Prep Tip on page 36). Set them aside.

2. In a large skillet, combine the butter and olive oil, and allow them to melt over medium-low heat. Add the corn and mix thoroughly. Increase the heat to medium. Add the sugar (if using), and the salt and pepper to taste. Stir, and allow to cook for 15 to 20 minutes. Remove from the heat, and enjoy.

INGREDIENT TIP: As a time saver, feel free to use frozen white corn kernels instead of cutting the kernels from fresh ears of corn. For a healthier, vegan, dairy-free version, eliminate the butter.

HEARTY POTATO SOUP

Serves 4 to 6

Prep time: 5 minutes / **Cook time:** 25 minutes

NUT-FREE, SOY-FREE, ONE-POT, UNDER 30

For generations, hearty potato soup has been a true comfort in homes across the South. This recipe, passed down from my great-grandmother, is one that we still enjoy today. The creaminess added to the cheesiness is what makes this dish so delicious, and a bit of a treat; a little bit goes a long way. My version of this soup uses small, diced potatoes simmered until the potatoes have broken down to achieve a smooth consistency. If you like a chunkier finish, start with larger chunks of potatoes.

2 tablespoons olive oil

1 yellow onion, finely diced

1 tablespoon minced garlic

4 tablespoons (½ stick) salted butter

½ cup all-purpose flour

2 pounds russet potatoes, peeled and diced

4 cups vegetable broth

1 cup whole milk

1 cup heavy whipping cream

2 teaspoons onion powder

Kosher salt

Ground black pepper

2 cups shredded Cheddar cheese

1. In a large pot, heat the oil over medium-low heat. Add the onion and stir, cooking for 2 to 3 minutes. Add the garlic and stir for an additional 1 minute. Add the butter and, when melted, whisk in flour until well combined.

2. To the same pot, add the potatoes, vegetable broth, milk, heavy whipping cream, onion powder, and salt and pepper to taste. Simmer, covered, for 15 minutes.

3. Stir in the cheese until it is completely melted, 2 to 3 minutes. Serve warm.

SUBSTITUTION TIP: This soup can be topped with numerous additions, such as sour cream, chopped green onions, or fresh parsley for flavor.

BRUNSWICK STEW

Serves 6

Prep time: 10 minutes / **Cook time:** 1 hour and 40 minutes

GLUTEN-FREE, NUT-FREE, SOY-FREE, ONE-POT

Brunswick stew reportedly originated in a place called Brunswick, Georgia (though others try to claim its deliciousness as well), and has been passed down through generations of grandmothers. When I lived in Savannah a few years back, I had the pleasure of traveling to Brunswick to taste the stew in its original home—it was truly indescribable. It is traditionally made using chicken, pork, or beef, but omitting them hardly makes a dent in the full flavor. If you do want to include a heartier meat substitute, add some shredded jackfruit (see Substitution Tip below).

2 tablespoons unsalted butter

1 cup finely chopped yellow onions

3 cups diced tomatoes (about 3 large tomatoes)

1 cup tomato juice

2 cups lima beans, fresh or frozen

2 cups corn kernels, fresh or frozen

8 cups vegetable broth

½ cup barbecue sauce (see Recipe Tip on page 42 for a homemade version)

1 tablespoon garlic powder

1 tablespoon onion powder

½ teaspoon red pepper flakes

Kosher salt

Ground black pepper

1. In a large pot, melt the butter over medium heat. Add the onions and stir, cooking for 3 to 4 minutes, until translucent. Add the tomatoes, tomato juice, lima beans, and corn, and mix thoroughly.

2. Add the broth, barbecue sauce, garlic powder, onion powder, red pepper flakes and salt and pepper to taste. Mix everything together. Cover with a lid, and allow to cook for 1½ hours over medium heat. Remove from the heat and enjoy warm, or freeze it and store it for up to 6 months.

SUBSTITUTION TIP: If you choose to add jackfruit, cook 2 cups shredded jackfruit in a skillet with grapeseed oil over medium heat, until it's golden brown and crispy, resembling chopped barbecue. Add it to the dish just before serving.

SAVORY STEWED TOMATOES

Serves 6

Prep time: 10 minutes / **Cook time:** 2 hours and 5 minutes

DAIRY-FREE, GLUTEN-FREE, NUT-FREE, SOY-FREE, VEGAN,
5-INGREDIENT, ONE-POT

My mom would make this recipe after Sunday church services. It was the perfect ending to the day and a great start to the week. This family favorite is a healthy version of the old-fashioned yet extremely popular Southern classic dish. Also known as tomato pudding for its smooth consistency, this delicate, rich recipe is packed with flavor and nutrients. This dish can be served as a main entrée with a corn bread side, over biscuits, or paired with okra and rice.

2 tablespoons olive oil

2 yellow onions, finely diced

2 garlic cloves, minced

10 large beefsteak and green (mixed) tomatoes, diced

1 tablespoon onion powder

Kosher salt

Ground black pepper

1. In a pot, heat the olive oil over medium heat. Add the onions and stir, cooking for 3 to 4 minutes, or until translucent.

2. Reduce the heat to medium-low. Add the garlic and stir for up to 1 minute, until fragrant. Add the tomatoes and mix thoroughly. Season with the onion powder, and salt and pepper to taste.

3. Allow the stew to simmer over medium-low heat for at least 2 hours, stirring occasionally. After 2 hours, taste and adjust the seasonings as necessary. Remove from the heat, and enjoy.

PREP TIP: This stew can be cooked for up to 6 hours and could alternatively be cooked in a crockpot. The longer it cooks, the smoother the consistency will be. If you use a crockpot, add all ingredients before sealing the crockpot, so the flavors mix well. For a faster alternative, cook it in a pressure cooker for about 30 minutes.

PINTO BEAN SOUP

Serves 4 to 6

Prep time: 5 minutes / **Cook time:** 30 minutes

DAIRY-FREE, GLUTEN-FREE, NUT-FREE, SOY-FREE, VEGAN, ONE-POT

This recipe makes a deliciously thick and creamy soup full of smoky, savory flavors, perfect for lunch or dinner. Pinto beans are heart healthy, and are known to help regulate blood sugar levels. Traditionally, this soup was made with ham hock for extra flavor, but I am confident that this vegetarian version needs no flavor boost.

2 tablespoons olive oil

2 yellow onions, sliced

1 green bell pepper, diced

1 garlic clove, finely diced

6 cups water

2 bay leaves

4 (15-ounce) cans pinto beans, drained and rinsed, or 2 cups dried pinto beans (see Ingredient Tip below)

1 teaspoon cayenne pepper

½ teaspoon ground cumin

Kosher salt

Ground black pepper

1. In a large pot, heat the olive oil over medium heat. Add the onions and bell pepper, and sauté for 2 to 3 minutes until browned. Add the garlic, and stir for 1 minute, until fragrant.

2. Pour in the water, stir, and add the bay leaves to the pot. Add the beans, cayenne pepper, cumin, and salt and pepper to taste. Stir everything together, and cover with a lid. Bring the soup to a simmer, then allow it to simmer over low heat for 25 minutes, or until the beans are soft.

INGREDIENT TIP: If you choose to use dried pinto beans, cover them with water and allow them to soak for 30 minutes before starting. Then follow the recipe as instructed, but boil the soup for 2 hours instead of 25 minutes.

HOMEMADE DUMPLINGS

Serves 4

Prep time: 15 minutes / **Cook time:** 30 minutes

NUT-FREE, SOY-FREE, ONE-POT

Nothing says comfort and soul like homemade dumplings. Soul food dumplings, unlike Chinese ones, for instance, have no filling. They use just the humble ingredients available traditionally, flour and water (well, now veggie broth). With just these few ingredients, the dumplings are guaranteed to have your home filled with warmth and delicious aromas. They can be prepared using just about any liquid, but for maximum flavor—and some vitamins and minerals—I use a broth just chock-full of fresh vegetables.

4¾ cups vegetable broth, divided

4 cups water

1 cup diced yellow onions

1 cup chopped celery

1 cup diced green bell pepper

3 garlic cloves, minced

2 teaspoons ground black pepper

2 kosher teaspoons salt, optional

2 cups self-rising flour, plus more for the surface

4 tablespoons (½ stick) unsalted butter, softened

1. In a large pot, combine 4 cups of the vegetable broth, the water, onions, celery, bell pepper, garlic, pepper, and salt (if using). Bring to a boil, then allow to simmer over medium heat for 10 minutes.

2. While the broth is cooking, in a medium mixing bowl, combine the flour and butter. Mix them together with your hands until a dough forms. Slowly add in the remaining ¾ cup of broth, and mix with your hands until well combined.

3. Place the dough on a floured surface. Knead for about 2 minutes, then flatten the dough with a floured rolling pin until it is 1 inch thick. Cut it into 2-inch squares.

4. Carefully place each piece of dough into the simmering pot of broth. Be sure not to stack the dumplings in the pot. Add the dumplings one by one to prevent them from sticking together. Allow them to cook in the broth over medium heat for at least 20 minutes.

5. Remove the soup from the heat, and allow to sit uncovered until ready to eat.

SUBSTITUTION TIP: For a thicker broth, mix in 1 tablespoon cornstarch 5 minutes before the dish is ready. Stir, and allow it to cook for the remaining 5 minutes. It will continue to thicken after it is removed from the heat.

CHEESY BROCCOLI SOUP

Serves 4 to 6

Prep time: 10 minutes / **Cook time:** 20 minutes

NUT-FREE, SOY-FREE, ONE-POT, UNDER 30

The warmth and comfort of this indulgent dish warms the soul on those chilly nights. It's especially popular during the winter holidays. In this recipe the sauce for the soup comes from fresh ingredients rather than the canned Cheddar cheese soup shortcut frequently used when making this dish.

4 tablespoons (½ stick) unsalted butter

2 carrots, grated

1 yellow onion, diced

2 garlic cloves, minced

½ cup all-purpose flour

2 heads broccoli, chopped into florets

4 cups vegetable broth

2 cups heavy whipping cream

1 cup shredded mild Cheddar cheese

1 cup shredded sharp Cheddar cheese

1 tablespoon onion powder

Kosher salt

Ground black pepper

1. In a large pot, melt the butter over medium-low heat. When the butter is melted, add the carrots and onion, stir, and cook for 3 to 4 minutes. Add the garlic, and stir for an additional 1 minute. Whisk in the flour until it is well incorporated.

2. Add the broccoli and the broth, and bring to a boil. Reduce the heat to low, cover, and continue to cook for an additional 10 minutes.

3. Add the heavy whipping cream, both types of Cheddar, onion powder, and salt and pepper to taste, and stir until the cheese has fully melted, 2 to 3 minutes. Adjust seasonings to taste, remove from the heat, and enjoy.

INGREDIENT TIP: To save time, feel free to use frozen broccoli florets. As an alternative, if you would like to avoid cooking on the stove, combine all the ingredients in a crockpot, and cook on high for 4 hours.

OKRA GUMBO REMIX

Serves 4

Prep time: 10 minutes / **Cook time:** 25 minutes

DAIRY-FREE, GLUTEN-FREE, NUT-FREE, SOY-FREE, VEGAN, ONE-POT

From the Bayou to your home, okra gumbo is packed with flavor and color. Okra, a staple of soul food brought over from Africa and planted by enslaved people, is full of fiber, vitamins, and minerals. In fact, the Tiwi (African language) name for okra, "ngombo," ultimately became the word "gumbo" in English. Which makes perfect sense because okra is the tasty thickening base that makes gumbo gumbo.

2 tablespoons olive oil

1 yellow onion, chopped

2 garlic cloves, chopped

3 beefsteak tomatoes, chopped

3 cups fresh (see Ingredient Tip below) or frozen and thawed okra, roughly chopped

1 cup tomato juice

1 cup corn kernels

½ teaspoon dried oregano

½ teaspoon white pepper

¼ teaspoon cayenne pepper

¼ teaspoon smoked paprika

Kosher salt

1. In a large skillet, heat the olive oil over medium heat. Add the onion, and cook for 2 to 3 minutes until translucent. Add the garlic, and stir continuously for up to 1 minute, until fragrant. Stir in the tomatoes and okra. Allow to cook for 10 minutes, stirring occasionally until blended smoothly.

2. Stir in the tomato juice, corn kernels, oregano, white pepper, cayenne pepper, paprika, and salt to taste. Allow it to cook over medium heat for an additional 10 minutes. Remove from the heat, taste, and adjust seasonings as necessary.

PREP TIP: This gumbo can be prepared well in advance and stored in the freezer for up to 6 months. When freezing, be sure to store it in an airtight container.

INGREDIENT TIP: If you're using fresh okra, to remove some of the slime prior to cooking, sauté the chopped okra alone in 1 tablespoon of olive oil for 4 to 5 minutes. Then add it to the stew in step 1 above.

BLACK-EYED PEA SOUP

Serves 6

Prep time: 10 minutes, plus 8 hours to soak / **Cook time:** 1 hour and 35 minutes

DAIRY-FREE, GLUTEN-FREE, NUT-FREE, SOY-FREE, VEGAN, ONE-POT

Black-eyed peas are considered a symbol of luck among soul food devotees. Dense and meaty, these Southern favorites are the perfect base for a filling, tasty, and healthy soup. Traditionally, this soup has been made using ham hocks and canned beans, but over time the recipe has evolved tremendously with the use of fresh ingredients with lower amounts of sodium. And in this vegetarian version, you won't miss the ham hock one bit.

2 cups dried black-eyed peas

2 tablespoons olive oil

1 large yellow onion, finely diced

1 green bell pepper, diced

1 garlic clove, finely diced

6 cups water

2 bay leaves

1 vegetable bouillon cube

1 teaspoon smoked paprika

¼ teaspoon dried thyme

¼ teaspoon ground cumin

Kosher salt

Ground black pepper

3 cups corn kernels

1. Prepare the black-eyed peas by covering them in water and allowing them to soak in a covered container on the counter for at least 8 hours.

2. In a large stockpot, heat the oil over medium heat. Add the onion, bell pepper, and garlic, and stir continuously for 2 to 3 minutes. Add the soaked black-eyed peas, water, bay leaves, bouillon cube, paprika, thyme, cumin, and salt and pepper to taste, and mix thoroughly. Allow the soup to cook for at least 1½ hours over medium heat. Taste, and adjust the seasonings as necessary.

3. In the last 10 minutes of cooking, add in the corn. Remove from the heat, and serve while warm.

INGREDIENT TIP: For faster cooking and no soaking time, substitute the dried peas with 2 (15-ounce) cans of black-eyed peas, drained and rinsed. If using canned peas, reduce cooking time to 30 minutes.

TANGY GREEN TOMATO SOUP

Serves 6

Prep time: 10 minutes / **Cook time:** 45 minutes

DAIRY-FREE, GLUTEN-FREE, NUT-FREE, SOY-FREE, VEGAN, ONE-POT

Green tomatoes are actually underripe tomatoes, but they are a staple of Southern cooking. When fried, these crunchy, tart, tangy vegetables are viewed as one of the most iconic soul food dishes in the South. But they should not be limited to their fried version. Here is a different take on this traditional soul food veggie: green tomato soup, the ultimate savory meal.

2 tablespoons olive oil
1 yellow onion, diced
2 garlic cloves, minced
4 cups vegetable broth
6 large green tomatoes, peeled and chopped into chunks

2 large beefsteak tomatoes, peeled and chopped into chunks
1 celery stalk, chopped
½ teaspoon cayenne pepper

Kosher salt
Ground black pepper
1 teaspoon liquid smoke

1. In a large pot, heat the oil over medium heat. Add the onion and garlic, and stir continuously for 1 to 2 minutes, or until the garlic becomes fragrant.

2. Pour in the vegetable broth and stir. Add the tomatoes, celery, cayenne pepper, and salt and pepper to taste, and stir. Cover with a lid, and bring it to a boil. Once boiling, reduce the heat to low, and simmer for 25 minutes.

3. Use an immersion blender (or pour soup into food processor) and blend until smooth. Pour the soup back into the pot, if necessary. Add the liquid smoke, then simmer over low heat for 5 to 10 minutes. Remove from the heat, and serve.

PREP TIP: This soup really comes alive when it is paired with Honey Butter Corn Bread (page 94) or Hush Puppies (page 99).

EAT YOUR COLLARD GREENS SOUP

Serves 6

Prep time: 10 minutes / **Cook time:** 1 hour and 25 minutes

DAIRY-FREE, GLUTEN-FREE, NUT-FREE, SOY-FREE, VEGAN, ONE-POT

Collard greens—famously a staple of soul food cooking, a member of the cabbage family, and the official vegetable of South Carolina—taste mild and earthy. They stand out in this filling, nourishing soup just packed with fresh vegetables and flavorful juices. Collard greens traditionally take a back (or side) seat to flashier main dishes on holidays. But for this recipe, the collards carry their own. The red pepper flakes add just that perfect touch of heat, but feel free to eliminate them if not to your taste.

2 tablespoons olive oil

1 cup diced carrot

1 white onion, diced

2 tablespoons minced
  garlic

1 bunch collard greens,
  de-stemmed and
  chopped

8 cups water

1 beefsteak tomato, diced

1 vegetable bouillon cube

1 tablespoon apple cider
  vinegar

1 teaspoon red pepper
  flakes, optional

Kosher salt

Ground black pepper

1. In a large pot, heat the olive oil over medium heat. Add the carrot and onion, and sauté for 1 to 2 minutes. Add the garlic and sauté for 1 minute, until the garlic is fragrant. Add the collard greens and stir continuously for 2 to 3 minutes.

2. Stir in the water, tomato, and vegetable bouillon. Cover with a lid, and allow to cook over medium heat for a minimum of 1 hour and 15 minutes. The collard green leaves will shrink.

3. After the soup has cooked, add the vinegar and red pepper flakes (if using), as well as salt and pepper to taste. Serve alone or alongside Honey Butter Corn Bread (page 94).

INGREDIENT TIP: To avoid having to clean, de-stem, and chop the collards, feel free to use frozen chopped collard greens. If using frozen collard greens, decrease the cook time in step 2 to 30 minutes. No need to thaw in advance.

MAINS

◀ FRIED MUSHROOM "CHICKEN," 74

VEGGIE-FULL POT PIE

Serves 4

Prep time: 15 minutes, plus 25 minutes to cool / **Cook time:** 45 minutes

NUT-FREE, SOY-FREE

What could be better than this delicious pie filled with vegetables in a creamy, well-seasoned sauce and topped with a flaky, buttery crust? Served on tables of Southern families for generations, and traditionally made with chicken, this veggie version loses absolutely nothing in the translation. In fact, it gains some vitamins and minerals. Whether using fresh or frozen veggies, the outcome of your pie flavors will be the same.

4 tablespoons (½ stick) unsalted butter

1 yellow onion, diced

4 garlic cloves, minced

1 russet potato, diced

1 cup sliced white mushrooms

1 cup diced fresh carrots

1 cup green peas

⅓ cup all-purpose flour

1½ cups heavy cream

1½ cups vegetable broth, plus more as needed

1 teaspoon dried thyme

Kosher salt

Ground black pepper

1 sheet puff pastry, thawed (or try the Multipurpose Pie Crust on page 105)

1 large egg, beaten, for egg wash

1. Preheat the oven to 400°F.

2. In a large skillet, melt the butter over medium heat. Add the onion and garlic, and cook for 1 to 2 minutes, continuously stirring to prevent the garlic from burning.

3. Add the potatoes and cook for 4 minutes, or until potatoes are soft. Add the mushrooms, carrots, and peas, and allow them to cook for an additional 4 minutes.

4. Stir in the flour, and allow the mixture to cook for 1 to 2 minutes, until thickened. Slowly pour in the heavy cream and broth, and stir until well combined. Add in the thyme, and salt and pepper to taste.

5. Bring to a low boil, reduce the heat to low, and simmer for 4 to 5 minutes until it becomes creamy. If the mixture becomes too thick, or the vegetables stick together, add in additional broth.

6. Remove from the heat, and pour the mixture into a 10-inch pie dish or any desired baking dish. Unroll the puff pastry and place it on top of the mixture. Seal the crust around the edges by pressing down slightly with a fork, forming a pie crust, then brush the top with the egg wash.

7. Cut 4 slits in the center of the crust, then place in the oven. Bake for 30 minutes, or until golden brown. Remove from the oven, and allow it to cool for at least 25 minutes. Then serve while the pie is warm.

NOT YOUR TYPICAL SHEPHERD'S PIE

Serves 4

Prep time: 10 minutes / **Cook time:** 40 minutes

NUT-FREE, SOY-FREE

Generally thought of as a British favorite, the American South has taken this recipe on and elevated it to a whole new level. This dish can stand on its own without any beef or lamb to distract from the fresh vegetables tossed in a rich, well-seasoned gravy, topped with mashed potatoes, and baked to perfection. This dish differs from the typical pot pie because there are many more veggies, and homemade mashed potatoes top the filling rather than puff pastry.

FOR THE TOPPING:

4 russet potatoes, peeled and chopped

1 tablespoon unsalted butter

2 tablespoons heavy whipping cream

Kosher salt

Ground black pepper

FOR THE FILLING:

2 (15-ounce) cans chickpeas, drained and rinsed

1 teaspoon Worcestershire sauce

1 tablespoon olive oil

1 tablespoon unsalted butter

1 yellow onion, finely diced

4 garlic cloves, finely diced

1 cup chopped white mushrooms

1 beefsteak tomato, finely diced and drained

1 cup chopped spinach

1 cup diced carrots

1 cup green peas

1 cup chopped broccoli

¼ cup vegetable broth

1 teaspoon dried thyme

1 teaspoon dried basil

1 teaspoon red pepper flakes

Kosher salt

Ground black pepper

2 tablespoons all-purpose flour

3 tablespoons heavy cream

1. Preheat the oven to 350°F.

2. **TO MAKE THE TOPPING:** In a large pot, cover the potatoes with cold water. Bring to a boil over high heat, and cook for 7 to 10 minutes, until soft.

3. Drain the water from the potatoes and place them in a large mixing bowl. Mash them with a potato masher until you reach a smooth consistency. Stir in the butter, whipping cream, and salt and pepper to taste. Set aside.

4. **TO MAKE THE FILLING:** Add the chickpeas and Worcestershire sauce to a small mixing bowl and mash with a fork or potato masher until smooth.

5. In a medium skillet, heat the olive oil and butter over medium heat. Add the onion and garlic, and cook for 1 to 2 minutes, continuously stirring. Add the mashed chickpeas, mushrooms, tomato, spinach, carrots, peas, and broccoli, and cook for 5 to 7 minutes, until softened.

6. Pour in the broth, and stir. Bring it to a low simmer, still over medium heat, for 2 minutes. Add the thyme, basil, red pepper flakes, and salt and pepper to taste, and mix thoroughly. Sprinkle in the flour, and stir until combined. Then add the heavy cream, and mix well until thickened.

7. Remove the skillet from the heat, and pour the contents into a 10-inch pie dish or casserole dish. Spread the mashed potato evenly on top, and place the dish in the oven. Bake for 10 to 15 minutes, or until golden brown.

SUBSTITUTION TIP: For a lower-carb version, use mashed cauliflower rather than mashed potatoes for the topping.

FRIED MUSHROOM "CHICKEN"

Serves 4

Prep time: 10 minutes / **Cook time:** 3 to 4 minutes per batch

NUT-FREE, SOY-FREE, ONE-PAN, UNDER 30

One of my mother's best meals, and a traditional soul food favorite, is her delicious fried chicken. The flavors and aromas bring back so many memories from my childhood, especially of Sunday dinners. But just because you're skipping the chicken doesn't mean you have to do away with the indulgent, delectable, crunchy, tasty, seasoned flavors of the traditional dish. Extra crispy with just a kick of heat, these fried mushrooms will fill the void and become a part of your regular meal roster for years to come.

32 ounces canola oil

2 cups all-purpose flour, divided

1 cup buttermilk

4 teaspoons onion powder, divided

4 teaspoons garlic powder, divided

2 teaspoons smoked paprika, divided

1 teaspoon sea salt

1 teaspoon cayenne pepper

1 pound oyster mushrooms, pulled into chicken-size pieces

1. In a cast iron or other large skillet, preheat the oil over medium heat to a temperature of 350°F (see Buffalo Oyster Po' Boy, Prep Tip, page 87).

2. In a medium bowl, prepare the wet batter by stirring together 1 cup of flour and the buttermilk. Add 2 teaspoons of the onion powder, 2 teaspoons of the garlic powder, 1 teaspoon of paprika, and the sea salt. Mix thoroughly and set aside.

3. In another medium bowl, prepare the dry batter by combining the remaining 1 cup of flour, 2 teaspoons of onion powder, 2 teaspoons of garlic powder, 1 teaspoon of paprika, and the cayenne pepper. Mix well.

4. Dip each chunk of mushroom into the wet batter, and then into the dry batter, and set aside until all mushrooms are coated.

5. Carefully add the mushrooms to the skillet with the preheated oil in batches, and fry for 3 to 4 minutes, or until golden brown. Remove, and set aside on a wire rack to cool. Enjoy alongside any meal.

INGREDIENT TIP: For a vegan and dairy-free alternative, use 1 cup of water instead of buttermilk in the wet batter.

SUBSTITUTION TIP: You can bake these on a baking sheet covered in parchment paper for a slightly less crunchy but healthier version. Just place coated mushrooms on the prepared baking sheet and bake at 400°F for 15 minutes, turning halfway through.

RED BEANS AND RICE MÉLANGE

Serves 4

Prep time: 10 minutes / **Cook time:** 50 minutes

Hailing from Louisiana, red beans and rice have become popular all over the South, especially in the area usually referred to as the Low Country. And it's no wonder. This healthy, hearty, naturally vegetarian dish is rich in flavor and just packed with protein. It's also a bit more kid-friendly, because I toned down the heat from the traditional version. Serve it with Hot Water Corn Bread (page 95) or Grandma's Biscuits (page 19) for that true Southern flair.

2 tablespoons olive oil

1 white onion, finely diced

1 green bell pepper, finely diced

3 garlic cloves, finely chopped

1 cup diced celery

2 teaspoons cayenne pepper

1 teaspoon dried thyme

1 teaspoon dried oregano

1 teaspoon chili powder

Kosher salt

Ground black pepper

2 (15-ounce) cans red kidney beans, drained and rinsed

4 cups vegetable broth

3 bay leaves

1 teaspoon cornstarch

2 cups cooked long-grain white rice (prepared to package instructions)

1. In a large pot, heat the oil over medium heat. Add the onion, bell pepper, and garlic, and cook for 2 to 3 minutes, stirring constantly until softened. Add the celery, and cook for an additional 2 minutes until tender. Add the cayenne pepper, thyme, oregano, chili powder, and salt and pepper to taste, and stir until well combined.

2. Add the red beans and broth, and stir well. Add the bay leaves, and cover with a lid. Bring it to a simmer for 40 minutes over medium heat, until the dish is very fragrant.

3. Add in the cornstarch, and stir for 2 minutes until the sauce thickens. Remove the bay leaves, and remove the pot from the heat. Serve alongside the cooked rice.

CHILI BEANS IN SMOKY SAUCE

Serves 6

Prep time: 10 minutes / **Cook time:** 1 hour and 35 minutes

DAIRY-FREE, GLUTEN-FREE, NUT-FREE, SOY-FREE, VEGAN, ONE-POT

There is little more satisfying on a cold fall or winter night than this chili bean recipe. On our family cabin trips, we perfected this dish to keep us cozy, warm, and full. Beans have been used in soul food dishes in the Deep South for centuries and are an excellent source of protein when you're skipping meat. Quinoa adds abundant nutrients like fiber and all 9 of the amino acids, along with its texture and mild nutty taste.

2 tablespoons olive oil

1 yellow onion, diced

1 green bell pepper, diced

1 tablespoon tomato paste

3 cups vegetable broth

3 (15-ounce) cans chili beans

½ cup quinoa

3 garlic cloves, minced

2 teaspoons unpacked light brown sugar

2 beefsteak tomatoes, diced

1 tablespoon smoked paprika

1 tablespoon ground cumin

1 tablespoon chili powder

1 bay leaf

Salt

1. In a Dutch oven, heat the oil over medium heat. Sauté the onion and bell pepper for 3 minutes, until onions are translucent. Add tomato paste and saute for 1 minute. Deglaze the pot by stirring in the vegetable broth, scraping from the bottom of the pot.

2. Add the beans, quinoa, garlic, brown sugar, tomatoes, paprika, cumin, chili powder, and bay leaf to the pot, and mix thoroughly. Cover with a lid, and allow to cook for 1 hour and 30 minutes, stirring occasionally.

3. Remove the bay leaf. Taste and adjust seasonings as needed. Add salt to taste. Remove from the heat, and serve while warm.

PREP TIP: This chili is best topped with shredded Cheddar cheese and served alongside Honey Butter Corn Bread (page 94).

CABBAGE AND POTATO SKILLET

Serves 4

Prep time: 10 minutes / **Cook time:** 20 minutes

GLUTEN-FREE, NUT-FREE, SOY-FREE, ONE-PAN, UNDER 30

Cabbage is one of those super-versatile, inexpensive, and always-available greens that have long been a crucial part of soul food and Southern cuisine. This one-pan cabbage extravaganza includes russet potatoes, which make the dish extra filling. Cabbage is traditionally served or seasoned with bacon or smoked turkey, but for this recipe, the flavorful vegetables and spices need no meaty accompaniment.

1 tablespoon olive oil	4 russet potatoes, diced	1 teaspoon dried basil
1 yellow onion, sliced	1 large head Napa	1 teaspoon red pepper
1 red bell pepper, sliced	cabbage, shredded	flakes
2 tablespoons salted	2 cups vegetable broth	Kosher salt
butter	1 teaspoon garlic powder	Ground black pepper

1. In a large skillet, heat the oil over medium heat. Add the onion and bell pepper, and cook for 2 to 3 minutes. Add the butter and potatoes to the skillet, and cook for 5 minutes, until potatoes have browned.

2. Add the cabbage and broth into the skillet and mix well. Add the garlic powder, basil, red pepper flakes, and salt and pepper to taste, and stir. Cover with a lid, and allow to cook for an additional 10 minutes, or until potatoes are soft. Serve warm.

INGREDIENT TIP: This recipe works with various types of cabbage, depending on your personal preference. Red (or purple) and green cabbage taste very similar to one another, but the red color can seep into any recipe you're making. Red cabbage contains more antioxidants than green cabbage. Napa cabbage is shaped differently, more oblong, than red or green cabbage, and is milder in taste. Savoy cabbage is a deeper green than green cabbage, and is less crispy and milder in taste.

RITZY SQUASH CASSEROLE

Serves 4 to 6

Prep time: 10 minutes / **Cook time:** 30 minutes

NUT-FREE

Squash casserole has many different variations and versions, depending on the family making it. This recipe is one that has been passed down through my family for generations. We use Ritz crackers because they're a family favorite, and their buttery flavor blends perfectly with the cheesy, bubbling casserole. But traditional bread crumbs in the same measure will work as well. Either way, you'll find the crunchy crust with the soft filling to be simply delectable.

Cooking spray

1 tablespoon olive oil

1 yellow onion, diced

2 pounds yellow squash, thinly sliced

1 teaspoon kosher salt

1 teaspoon ground black pepper

1 tablespoon unsalted butter

1 cup shredded Cheddar cheese

¾ cup grated Parmesan cheese

½ cup sour cream

2 cups crushed Ritz crackers

1. Preheat the oven to 350°F. Spray a 13-by-9-inch casserole dish with cooking spray.

2. In a skillet, heat the oil over medium heat. Add the onion and cook for 1 to 2 minutes, stirring. Add the squash, salt, pepper, and butter, and cook for 7 to 8 minutes, until the squash has softened.

3. Remove the skillet from the heat, and add the Cheddar and Parmesan cheeses, and the sour cream. Mix well. Pour the mixture into the prepared casserole dish, then top with the crushed crackers. Bake for 20 minutes, or until the crust is golden brown. Serve warm.

SUBSTITUTION TIP: For a twist on taste, color, and vitamins, make a zucchini and squash casserole. Use 1 pound of each, and follow the same recipe.

CHICKPEA "MEATLOAF"

Makes 1 loaf

Prep time: 15 minutes / **Cook time:** 35 minutes

DAIRY-FREE, NUT-FREE, SOY-FREE, VEGAN

Everyone has a family meatloaf recipe somewhere in the books. After all, it has always been an affordable, hearty, versatile, and satisfying meal. Now vegetarians don't need to feel left out. An excellent twist on regular meatloaf, this chickpea loaf is simple to make and just filled with flavor. The chickpeas offer a nutritious plant protein to replace the meat; plus, they don't contain unhealthy fats, are super filling, and are an excellent source of fiber.

FOR THE LOAF:

- 1 tablespoon olive oil
- 1 yellow onion, finely diced
- ½ cup finely diced carrots
- ½ green bell pepper, finely diced
- 3 garlic cloves, minced
- 2 (15-ounce) cans chickpeas, drained and rinsed
- 3 tablespoons hickory barbecue sauce (see Recipe Tip on page 42 for a homemade version)
- 1 tablespoon chopped fresh cilantro
- 1 teaspoon dried rosemary
- 1 teaspoon ground cumin
- 1 teaspoon kosher salt
- 1 teaspoon ground black pepper
- ¾ cup Italian-style bread crumbs

FOR THE GLAZE, OPTIONAL:

- ½ cup ketchup
- ½ cup barbecue sauce (see Recipe Tip on page 42 for a homemade version)
- 2 tablespoons unpacked brown sugar
- ½ teaspoon smoked paprika

1. Preheat the oven to 400°F. Line a 9-by-5-inch loaf pan with parchment paper, and set aside.

2. **TO MAKE THE LOAF:** In a medium skillet, heat the oil over medium heat. Add the onion, carrots, and bell pepper. Sauté for 3 to 4 minutes, until softened. Add the garlic, and allow it to cook for 1 minute, stirring, until fragrant. Remove from heat. Pour all of the cooked vegetables into the bowl of a food processor, and blend until smooth.

3. Add the chickpeas, barbecue sauce, and cilantro to the mixture already in the food processor, and blend together until smooth.

4. Pour the blended mixture into a large mixing bowl, and mix in the rosemary, cumin, salt, and pepper. Slowly add the bread crumbs, until the mixture reaches a thick consistency. If it's too dry, add a few tablespoons of water. Put the meatloaf mixture in the prepared loaf pan, forming it into a loaf, and either glaze it (step 5) or bake (step 6).

5. **TO MAKE THE OPTIONAL GLAZE**: In a medium bowl, stir together the ketchup, barbecue sauce, brown sugar, and paprika. Spread this glaze evenly over the meatloaf.

6. Bake for 30 minutes, or until browned. Serve warm.

SUBSTITUTION TIP: If you opt not to make the glaze, serve this simple "meatloaf" with your favorite meatloaf toppings, like ketchup, or with a side of mashed potatoes.

MUSHROOM GRAVY SMOTHERED BURGERS

Serves 4

Prep time: 15 minutes / **Cook time:** 1 hour

NUT-FREE, SOY-FREE

This delicious tender black bean burger smothered in a traditional brown gravy with a mushroom twist is the ultimate soul food Sunday meal. Let's be honest: Anything smothered in gravy is the ultimate meal. Here, I substitute black beans for ground beef, which have a similar texture. This veggie version of the traditional dish is a bit healthier but just as scrumptious and just as Southern.

FOR THE GRAVY:

Cooking spray

½ cup (1 stick) unsalted butter, softened

1 cup white mushrooms

¼ cup all-purpose flour

1¼ cups vegetable stock

1 teaspoon thyme

1 teaspoon kosher salt

1 teaspoon ground black pepper

½ teaspoon ground sage

FOR THE BURGERS:

1 tablespoon olive oil

½ cup diced onions

½ cup diced green bell pepper

1 (15-ounce) can black beans, drained and rinsed

2 garlic cloves, minced

3 tablespoons cornmeal

1 teaspoon kosher salt

1 teaspoon ground black pepper

1 teaspoon cayenne pepper

½ teaspoon chili powder

1. Preheat the oven to 350°F. Prepare a baking sheet by spraying it with cooking spray.

2. **TO MAKE THE GRAVY:** In a large skillet, melt the butter over medium-low heat. Add the mushrooms, and sauté for 15 minutes, until lightly browned and softened. Whisk in the flour until it is lightly browned and clumps form, about 5 minutes. Slowly whisk in the stock. Bring it to a low simmer for 5 to 7 minutes until the gravy has thickened. Add the thyme, salt, pepper, and sage, and stir. Adjust the seasonings to taste, remove from the heat, and set aside.

3. **TO MAKE THE BURGERS:** In a large skillet, heat the oil over medium heat. Add the onions and pepper, and sauté for 4 minutes, until onions are translucent.

4. Add the black beans, and stir until warm. Then remove the skillet from the heat, and transfer the warmed beans, onion, and bell pepper to a large mixing bowl.

5. To the mixing bowl with the beans, add the garlic, cornmeal, salt, black pepper, cayenne pepper, and chili powder, and mash everything together until smooth.

6. Form 4 patties using a ¼-cup measure, and place them on the prepared baking sheet. Bake for 15 minutes.

7. Flip the burgers over and carefully pour the gravy over the burgers. Place them back into the oven, and cook for an additional 15 minutes. They should be browned on both sides. Remove them from the oven and serve alone, on buns, over mashed potatoes, or with rice.

SUBSTITUTION TIP: It's so easy to make this recipe vegan (and non-dairy, for that matter). The burgers are already there. For the gravy, just replace the butter with a non-dairy or vegan butter alternative.

CREAMY KALE SKILLET

Serves 4

Prep time: 5 minutes / **Cook time:** 1 hour and 5 minutes

GLUTEN-FREE, NUT-FREE, SOY-FREE

Kale is so nutrient-dense, it can reduce your risk of cancer and lower your cholesterol. It is even said to help with weight loss because of its high water content. So, it's lucky that it is one of the greens so foundational to soul food. Related to collards and the cabbage family, kale has a slightly stronger, more bitter taste. But when cooked with just the right Southern touches, it becomes truly flavorful. This light skillet can be served alone or with a side of Hush Puppies (page 99).

2 cups cauliflower florets (from 1 small cauliflower)

2 tablespoons olive oil

1 small yellow onion, diced

2 bunches fresh curly kale, de-stemmed and chopped

1 teaspoon garlic powder

½ cup low-fat milk

Kosher salt

Ground black pepper

½ cup light sour cream

½ cup grated Parmesan cheese, divided

1. Preheat the oven to 350°F.

2. In a large pot, cover the cauliflower florets with water. Bring it to a boil, and cook for 10 to 12 minutes until softened. Drain, lightly mash, and set aside.

3. In a large cast iron (oven-safe) skillet, heat the oil over medium heat. Add the onion and cook for 3 minutes, stirring occasionally, until it's translucent.

4. Add the chopped kale and cook for 5 minutes, until wilted. Stir in the garlic powder, milk, and the salt and pepper to taste, and bring to a low boil for 5 minutes. While still over heat, add in the mashed cauliflower, sour cream, and half of the cheese. Mix thoroughly.

5. Take the skillet off the heat. Sprinkle the remaining cheese over the top of the mixture, cover the skillet with foil, and bake in the oven for 20 minutes. Remove the foil, and bake for 20 additional minutes until the cheese has a brown crust around the edges.

SUBSTITUTION TIP: Feel free to substitute potatoes for the cauliflower if desired.

VEGGIE JAMBALAYA

Serves 4

Prep time: 5 minutes / **Cook time:** 45 minutes

DAIRY-FREE, GLUTEN-FREE, NUT-FREE, SOY-FREE, VEGAN, ONE-POT

Let the good times roll with this veggie (and soul food and healthy) version of the Creole one-pot favorite, jambalaya. This twist on the Louisiana favorite uses veggies, spices, and of course, cabbage, to create a flavorful dish that could satisfy the crowds in any Second Line.

4 tablespoons olive oil, divided

2 yellow onions, diced

¼ cup diced celery

3 garlic cloves, minced

2 cups sliced portobello mushrooms

1 teaspoon garlic powder

1 teaspoon cayenne pepper

1 teaspoon onion powder

1 large head green cabbage, chopped

2 cups vegetable broth

2 small beefsteak tomatoes, diced

1 cup brown rice

Kosher salt

Ground black pepper

1. In a large pot, heat 2 tablespoons of olive oil over medium heat. Add the onions, celery, and garlic, and sauté for about 1 minute, until the garlic becomes fragrant.

2. Add the portobello mushrooms, the remaining 2 tablespoons of olive oil, the garlic powder, cayenne pepper, and onion powder, and mix thoroughly. Sear in the skillet over medium heat for 12 minutes.

3. Add the cabbage, broth, tomatoes, rice, and salt and pepper to taste, and stir until well combined. Cover the pot with a lid and allow it to cook over medium heat for at least 30 minutes, until the cabbage is soft. Serve with any sides you like.

PREP TIP: Before serving, be sure to let it cool for 5 to 10 minutes to prevent burns.

VARIATION TIP: Feel free to slice and sear a vegetarian sausage to add in if you find yourself wanting a slightly meatier dish.

BUFFALO OYSTER PO' BOY

Serves 4

Prep time: 10 minutes, plus 5 minutes to cool / **Cook time:** 5 minutes

NUT-FREE, SOY-FREE, ONE-PAN, UNDER 30

The "Po' Boy" originated in 1920s New Orleans to feed striking streetcar drivers ("poor boys"). It was initially made using the meat, oysters, or shrimp on hand at the time. Aside from the semantic overlap, *oyster* mushrooms, when cooked and seasoned to perfection, can have the same texture as chicken, making them the perfect veggie alternative for this Southern soul food classic. They can be tossed in any sauce, such as buffalo sauce, drizzled with ketchup, or served plain on hoagie rolls.

2 cups all-purpose flour, divided

1 cup buttermilk

4 teaspoons onion powder, divided

4 teaspoons garlic powder, divided

2 teaspoons smoked paprika, divided

1 teaspoon sea salt

1 teaspoon cayenne pepper

1 pound oyster mushrooms, cut into chunks

32 ounces canola oil

1 cup store-bought buffalo sauce

4 hoagie rolls, for serving

4 tomato slices, for serving

4 lettuce leaves, for serving

1. In a medium mixing bowl, prepare the wet batter by stirring together 1 cup of flour and the buttermilk. Add 2 teaspoons of onion powder, 2 teaspoons of garlic powder, 1 teaspoon of paprika, and the sea salt. Mix thoroughly and set aside.

2. In another medium mixing bowl, prepare the dry batter by thoroughly mixing the remaining flour, onion powder, garlic powder, and paprika, as well as the salt and cayenne pepper.

3. Dip each chunk of mushroom into the wet batter and then into the dry batter, and set aside on a plate until all mushrooms are coated.

4. Preheat the canola oil in a cast iron or large skillet until the temperature reads 350°F (see Prep Tip below).

5. Carefully add the mushrooms into the oil, and fry for 3 to 4 minutes, or until golden brown. Remove and set them aside on a wire rack to cool for 5 minutes.

6. Once cool, toss the fried mushrooms in the buffalo sauce until the pieces are fully coated. Assemble your sandwiches on hoagie rolls, using the buffalo oysters, tomato, and lettuce.

SUBSTITUTION TIP: Fried oyster mushrooms can be tossed into any sauce of your choice. Instead of buffalo sauce, feel free to toss them in barbecue sauce or your favorite dipping sauce.

PREP TIP: If you do not have a thermometer, dip a toothpick or the end of a wooden spoon in the hot oil. If the oil produces bubbles, then it is ready.

CHOPPED BARBECUE SLIDERS

Serves 4

Prep time: 10 minutes / **Cook time:** 10 minutes

DAIRY-FREE, NUT-FREE, SOY-FREE, VEGAN, ONE-PAN, UNDER 30

Barbecue in and of itself is a Southern tradition, especially among families in Georgia and North Carolina. Chopped barbecue sliders have been prepared using pork for years, but this veggie alternative using shredded jackfruit promises to be equally tasty and much healthier. You'll savor these mouth-watering sliders, because they are quick to whip up and full of flavor.

2 tablespoons olive oil

2 (20-ounce) cans jackfruit, shredded to resemble chopped barbecue

2 cups barbecue sauce (see Recipe Tip on page 42 for a homemade version)

1 teaspoon smoked paprika

1 teaspoon onion powder

1 teaspoon garlic powder

Kosher salt

Ground black pepper

12 slider buns

1 cup prepared coleslaw, optional

1. In a skillet, heat the oil over medium heat. Add the shredded jackfruit and cook for 5 to 6 minutes, stirring occasionally, until browned. Add the barbecue sauce, paprika, onion powder, garlic powder, and salt and pepper to taste. Stir until well combined, cook for 5 more minutes, then remove from the heat.

2. Serve the mixture on slider buns, and top (or accompany) with coleslaw, if using.

SUBSTITUTION TIP: For a twist, use 4 king oyster mushrooms instead of jackfruit. Simply chop and pan sear until the texture is darkened on the edges and resembles chopped barbecue, and then prepare the same way as the jackfruit. For a sweeter taste, use Hawaiian roll buns.

BROCCOLI RICE CASSEROLE

Serves 6

Prep time: 5 minutes / **Cook time:** 45 minutes

NUT-FREE, SOY-FREE

This creamy, cheesy comfort food has been prepared by generations of Southerners, traditionally using canned cream of chicken soup (and even Cheez Wiz or Velveeta) as a shortcut. This version prepares a fresh sauce that packs ten times the flavor, so you'll enjoy the indulgence even more. It's a great dish to bring to cookouts, reunions, or church lunches because it easily serves large crowds. Feel free to use fresh or frozen broccoli (see Ingredient Tip below).

Cooking spray

2 tablespoons unsalted butter

2 tablespoons all-purpose flour

1 cup heavy cream

½ (8-ounce) package cream cheese, softened

3 heads broccoli, chopped (about 6 cups)

1 garlic clove, minced

Kosher salt

Ground black pepper

1 cup shredded Cheddar cheese, divided

2 cups cooked white rice

1. Preheat the oven to 350°F. Coat a 9-by-11-inch casserole dish with cooking spray.

2. In a large skillet, melt the butter over medium heat. Stir in the flour until smooth, about 1 minute. Slowly add the heavy cream and bring it to a low simmer. Cook for 3 to 4 minutes, stirring constantly. Add the cream cheese, and stir until melted and well combined. Add in the broccoli, garlic, salt and pepper to taste, and half of the shredded cheese. Stir until well combined.

3. Combine with the rice and pour the mixture into the prepared casserole dish, and top with the remaining cheese. Bake for 35 minutes or until golden brown, and serve warm.

INGREDIENT TIP: If using frozen broccoli, be sure to thaw it before adding it to the dish.

COLLARD PILAU

Serves 6

Prep time: 10 minutes / **Cook time:** 20 minutes

DAIRY-FREE, GLUTEN-FREE, NUT-FREE, SOY-FREE, VEGAN, ONE-POT, UNDER 30

Pilau is a traditional rice-based soul food dish. It generally features a mix of rice, chicken, and bacon grease, but here, we will substitute heart-healthy olive oil for the grease and hearty collard greens for the chicken. If you serve this dish with black-eyed peas, it becomes a traditional New Year's meal eaten by African American families across the country. It has been said to bring good financial luck into the new year. These meals have a deep history, having been cooked and eaten since the antebellum era in the South.

2 tablespoons olive oil

1 yellow onion, diced

2 cups shredded jackfruit

1 teaspoon smoked paprika

1 teaspoon garlic powder

1 bunch collard greens, de-stemmed and chopped

½ cup vegetable broth

2 cups corn kernels

1 teaspoon white vinegar

1 teaspoon red pepper flakes

1 teaspoon kosher salt

1 teaspoon ground black pepper

1 cup cooked white rice (prepared to package instructions)

1. In a large pot, heat the olive oil over medium heat. Add the onion, shredded jackfruit, paprika, and garlic powder, and stir well. Cook for 3 to 4 minutes, until the onions are translucent.

2. Add the collard greens and sauté until wilted, about 6 minutes. Add the broth, corn, vinegar, red pepper flakes, salt, and pepper, and stir. Bring to a low simmer for 10 minutes.

3. Add the cooked rice. Mix together, remove the dish from heat, and serve.

INGREDIENT TIP: For a faster prep alternative, use pre-chopped frozen and thawed collards. For rice, boil-in-bag is a simple solution for a quick meal.

RICE PERLO

Serves 6

Prep time: 5 minutes / **Cook time:** 40 minutes

DAIRY-FREE, GLUTEN-FREE, NUT-FREE, SOY-FREE, VEGAN, ONE-POT

Perlo is an historical dish of the Carolinas, specifically Charleston, generally referring to a steamed rice dish with chicken. The delicious twist here is that it contains rice, beans, and fresh vegetables instead of the usual poultry. The seasonings of the vegetable broth and flavors from the rice blend perfectly to give you a satisfying soupy but thick texture that tastes superb.

1 tablespoon olive oil

1 yellow onion, diced

1 garlic clove, minced

1½ cups vegetable broth

1 (15-ounce) can black beans, drained and rinsed

1 cup white rice

1 cup water

1 beefsteak tomato, diced

Kosher salt

Ground black pepper

1. Preheat the oven to 350°F.

2. In a Dutch oven or oven-safe pot, heat the oil over medium heat. Add the onion and garlic, and sauté for 1 minute. Add the vegetable broth, beans, rice, water, tomato, and salt and pepper to taste, and mix until well combined. Bring to a low boil, then turn off the heat. The whole process will take about 10 minutes.

3. Place the pot into the oven, and bake for about 30 minutes, until the rice is fluffy and done. Serve warm.

COZY APPLE COBBLER, 106

CHAPTER 6

DESSERTS, BREADS, BISCUITS, AND GRAVY

HONEY BUTTER CORN BREAD

Serves 8

Prep time: 10 minutes / **Bake time:** 20 minutes

NUT-FREE, SOY-FREE, ONE-PAN, UNDER 30

Every true Southern cook has a time-tested corn bread recipe. After all, it is a staple in Southern kitchens and can be paired with just about any soul food dish. Corn bread was originally made by enslaved chefs who received inexpensive cornmeal as part of their rations. They learned to use the corn from Native Americans, who had been using it for generations. Serve this corn bread with Vegan Collard Greens (page 34).

1 cup yellow cornmeal

1 cup all-purpose flour

½ cup granulated white sugar

1 teaspoon baking powder

½ teaspoon baking soda

1 cup buttermilk

¼ cup plus 2 tablespoons honey, plus more for drizzling

2 large eggs, beaten

1 tablespoon ground cinnamon

8 tablespoons (1 stick) salted butter, melted

Cooking spray

1. Preheat the oven to 400°F.

2. In a large mixing bowl, whisk together the cornmeal, flour, sugar, baking powder, and baking soda until blended. In the center of the cornmeal mixture, pour the buttermilk, honey, eggs, and cinnamon. Mix together thoroughly. Add the butter and stir gently until incorporated.

3. Spray an oven-safe, 10-inch cast-iron skillet with cooking spray, and place it into the preheated oven to heat up for 5 minutes. When the skillet is warm, remove it from oven, and pour the batter in. Put it back in the oven, and bake for about 20 minutes, or until browned to your liking. Remove it from the oven, and drizzle with additional honey.

INGREDIENT TIP: Feel free to omit the sugar if you enjoy a more savory version of corn bread. Make an extra batch so that you can make Corn Bread Dressing (page 96).

HOT WATER CORN BREAD

Serves 4

Prep time: 5 minutes / **Cook time:** 20 minutes

DAIRY-FREE, GLUTEN-FREE, NUT-FREE, SOY-FREE, VEGAN,
5-INGREDIENT, ONE-PAN, UNDER 30

Hot water corn bread is also rooted in the history and creativity of enslaved cooks with Native American influences, when cornmeal was cheap and readily available. It is a different take on baked corn bread. This type of corn bread offers a crispy, crunchy crust while the center yields that same moist fluffy texture as traditional corn bread. Serve it with Vegan Collard Greens (page 34) and Red Beans and Rice Mélange (page 76).

3 cups canola oil

2 cups yellow cornmeal

¾ cup granulated white
    sugar

1 teaspoon kosher salt

1 teaspoon baking powder

1 cup boiling water

1. In a skillet, preheat the oil to 350°F (see Buffalo Oyster Po' Boy, Prep Tip, page 87).

2. In a medium, heat-safe mixing bowl, combine the cornmeal, sugar, salt, and baking powder. Slowly stir in the boiling water to create a batter. Form the batter into about 8 palm-size patties.

3. Carefully drop 4 patties into the hot oil and fry for 5 minutes on each side until golden brown. Repeat and fry the next batch of 4 to avoid overcrowding the skillet.

4. Remove the corn bread patties from the oil, and set them aside on paper towels to drain the excess oil. Serve while warm.

SUBSTITUTION TIP: Add some jalapeños to this corn bread for a bit of a spicy kick.

CORN BREAD DRESSING

Serves 8

Prep time: 10 minutes / **Cook time:** 40 minutes

NUT-FREE, SOY-FREE

This popular holiday soul food dish is called "dressing" in the South, but if you come from northern states, you might call it stuffing. That said, the two dishes aren't exactly the same: Stuffing is generally made using bread crumbs, but dressing is made using leftover corn bread, which adds so much more Southern flair. The other major difference is that stuffing is traditionally "stuffed" inside of a turkey and cooked, and dressing is a stand-alone dish baked in its own pan.

Cooking spray

4 tablespoons (½ stick) salted butter

1 yellow onion, finely diced

¾ cup finely diced celery

2 cups vegetable broth, plus more as needed

4 cups crumbled Honey Butter Corn Bread (page 94)

3 large eggs, beaten

1 tablespoon dried sage

1 teaspoon dried thyme

Kosher salt

Ground black pepper

1. Preheat the oven to 350°F. Prepare a 9-by-13-inch baking dish by spraying it with cooking spray.

2. In a large skillet, melt the butter over medium heat. Add the onion and celery, and sauté for 5 to 6 minutes or until translucent. Add the broth, cover the skillet, and bring it to a boil. Cook for 5 minutes.

3. In a large mixing bowl, mix together the corn bread, eggs, sage, thyme, and salt and pepper to taste. Add the cooked onions and celery, and combine. Add additional broth if the mixture is too dry.

4. Pour the mixture into the prepared dish, and bake for 30 minutes or until browned. Serve warm.

STICKY GOOEY BREAD PUDDING

Serves 6

Prep time: 5 minutes, plus 15 minutes to soak and rest / **Cook time:** 50 minutes

NUT-FREE, SOY-FREE

Southern cuisine has taken on this European classic as its own because of its indulgence and frugality. It's indulgent because of its gooey, sweet, warm goodness. It's frugal because it uses day-old bread otherwise destined for the compost pile. So, on those days where you realize your bread has become stale but you're in the mood to indulge, just throw together this quick dessert, and your family will be thrilled.

Cooking spray
8 slices day-old sandwich
   bread (4 cups cubed)
   (see Ingredient Tip
   below)
½ cup raisins, optional

¼ cup salted butter
2½ cups whole milk
2 eggs, beaten
¾ cup granulated white
   sugar

1 tablespoon pure vanilla
   extract
½ teaspoon ground
   cinnamon
½ teaspoon ground
   nutmeg

1. Preheat the oven to 350°F. Grease a 9-inch-square casserole dish with cooking spray and set aside.

2. In a large mixing bowl, combine the bread and the raisins (if using). Set aside.

3. In a saucepan, melt the butter over medium heat. Stir in the milk, and bring it to a simmer. Allow it to simmer for 4 to 5 minutes, until the milk is bubbling.

4. Pour the hot mixture over the bread and raisins, and mix thoroughly. Allow to soak for at least 5 minutes, then mix in the eggs, sugar, vanilla, cinnamon, and nutmeg.

5. Pour the mixture into the prepared casserole dish, and bake for 45 minutes. You'll know it's done when you insert a knife and it comes out clean. Remove from the oven, and allow it to rest for about 10 minutes before serving.

INGREDIENT TIP: You are welcome to use any type of bread as long as it is "day-old" or just past its expiration date. Sandwich bread, brioche, challah, old donuts—any bread will work perfectly for this recipe.

SWEET POTATO BISCUITS

Serves 8

Prep time: 15 minutes / **Bake time:** 12 minutes

NUT-FREE, SOY-FREE, 5-INGREDIENT, UNDER 30

Just thinking about these sweet potato biscuits makes my mouth water, so it's no surprise that they have been enjoyed in homes across the South for over 100 years. Famously called "Sunday Morning Biscuits," these next-level biscuits can be enjoyed during breakfast, lunch, and dinner, on any day of the week.

2 cups self-rising flour, plus more for surface

1 teaspoon kosher salt

½ teaspoon allspice

8 tablespoons (1 stick) unsalted butter, cold and finely grated

1 cup (from 1 potato) mashed cooked sweet potato (see Potato Cakes for mashed potato instructions, page 30)

½ cup buttermilk

1. Preheat the oven to 400°F. Prepare a baking sheet with parchment paper.

2. In a large mixing bowl, combine the flour, salt, and allspice. Knead in the grated butter using a pastry cutter or two forks until the butter is well combined with the flour. Add the mashed sweet potatoes and buttermilk, and mix thoroughly.

3. Place the dough onto a floured surface, and flatten. Cut it using a 2- or 3-inch biscuit cutter. Place the biscuits on the prepared baking sheet, and bake for 12 minutes or until the bottoms are golden brown. Serve immediately.

INGREDIENT TIP: Sweet potatoes are used in this dish for their color and taste. Yams, though also common in soul food cooking, are slightly starchier and do not have the sweetness of sweet potatoes.

HUSH PUPPIES

Serves 4

Prep time: 5 minutes / **Cook time:** 10 minutes

Hush puppies date back to the antebellum era. During that time period, enslaved individuals threw these warm fried bread bites at the guard dogs to silence them from howling when they were attempting to escape. Hush puppies are made of cornmeal and are served alongside many soul food meals, especially fried fish, fried shrimp, and fried chicken dinners. They are ubiquitous on menus in restaurants across the South. Try them alongside Fried Mushroom "Chicken" (page 74).

2 cups canola oil

1 cup yellow cornmeal

½ cup all-purpose flour

2 tablespoons granulated white sugar

1 teaspoon baking powder

1 teaspoon kosher salt

½ teaspoon garlic powder

½ cup buttermilk

¼ cup melted unsalted butter

1 large egg, beaten

2 tablespoons finely diced onion

1. In a large cast-iron skillet, preheat the oil to 350°F (see Buffalo Oyster Po' Boy, Prep Tip, page 87).

2. In a large mixing bowl, thoroughly whisk together the cornmeal, flour, sugar, baking powder, salt, and garlic powder. Slowly whisk in the buttermilk and melted butter, followed by the beaten egg, and finally the onion.

3. Drop 2-tablespoon-size balls of batter into the preheated oil. Cook them in two separate batches of 8 to prevent overcrowding the skillet. Fry for 3 to 4 minutes, or until golden brown. Remove from the oil and let them drain on paper towels before serving warm.

MOM'S HOMEMADE MOLASSES

Serves 6

Prep time: 5 minutes / **Cook time:** 5 minutes

DAIRY-FREE, GLUTEN-FREE, NUT-FREE, SOY-FREE,
5-INGREDIENT, ONE-PAN, UNDER 30

Molasses is a traditional topping for several soul food meals. It is also sometimes used as a sweetening agent in bread and dessert recipes. Homemade molasses has a uniquely superior and fresher taste than store-bought. And it's worth the little bit of labor, because it can be made in under 10 minutes. Try it on Sweet Potato Biscuits (page 98).

1 cup unpacked dark
  brown sugar

¾ cup honey
¼ cup water

1 teaspoon freshly
  squeezed lemon juice

In a medium skillet, combine the brown sugar, honey, water, and lemon juice, and heat over medium-low heat. Stir continuously for 5 minutes until well combined. Remove from the heat, and pour into a glass container or mason jar for storing.

PREP TIP: Molasses will last stored in a mason jar for up to 6 months—no need to refrigerate.

BROWN GRAVY EXTRAORDINAIRE

Serves 6

Prep time: 5 minutes / **Cook time:** 10 minutes

NUT-FREE, SOY-FREE, 5-INGREDIENT, ONE-PAN, UNDER 30

Gravy can be paired with just about any soul food dish and has long been a staple for enhancing flavors and textures. Traditionally prepared using the pan drippings from cooked chicken and other meats, this recipe kicks up the freshness and healthiness a notch by replacing the drippings with vegetable stock and ground thyme. This brown gravy is great served atop Chickpea "Meatloaf" (page 80).

½ cup unsalted butter, softened

¼ cup all-purpose flour

1¼ cups vegetable stock

1 teaspoon ground thyme

1 teaspoon kosher salt

1 teaspoon ground black pepper

1. In a medium skillet, melt the butter over low heat. Allow it to cook until lightly browned. Slowly whisk in the flour until well combined.

2. Slowly whisk in the vegetable stock, and raise the heat to medium-low. Bring the mixture to a low simmer for 5 to 7 minutes, or until the gravy has thickened.

3. Add the thyme, salt, and pepper, and adjust them to taste. Remove from the heat, and serve over whatever dish you choose.

SAWMILL GRAVY

Serves 4 to 6

Prep time: 5 minutes / **Cook time:** 15 minutes

NUT-FREE, SOY-FREE, ONE-PAN, UNDER 30

Sawmill gravy is white in color, a bit gritty in texture, and completely opposite in taste to traditional brown gravy. Sawmill gravy gained its name in the late 1800s because this dish was served primarily to sawmill workers and loggers to keep them full throughout their workdays. This gravy is a perfect example of the distinctive soul food "use what you've got" mentality. The traditional version uses meat drippings to enhance the flavor. The vegetarian version is often called "milk gravy." Either way, this gravy brings new life to Honey Corn Bread Waffles (page 21) and to my Grandma's Biscuits (page 19).

4 tablespoons (½ stick) salted butter

¼ cup all-purpose flour

2 cups whole milk

1 teaspoon kosher salt

1 teaspoon ground black pepper

1 teaspoon onion powder

1 teaspoon garlic powder

½ teaspoon cayenne pepper

¼ teaspoon rubbed sage

1. In a medium skillet, melt the butter over medium-low heat. Whisk in the flour until well combined. Slowly whisk in the milk until the mixture reaches a smooth consistency, about 5 minutes.

2. Add the salt, pepper, onion powder, garlic powder, cayenne pepper, and sage. Taste, and adjust seasonings accordingly. Bring the gravy to a low simmer for 5 minutes, whisking consistently to prevent burning.

3. Remove it from the heat when it reaches a smooth consistency. Serve immediately with your desired dish.

PREP TIP: This gravy can be stored in portion-size storage bags in the freezer for 3 to 6 months.

TANGY TOMATO GRAVY

Serves 4 to 6

Prep time: 10 minutes / **Cook time:** 15 minutes

NUT-FREE, SOY-FREE, ONE-PAN, UNDER 30

Tomato gravy is another staple of soul food that stems from ingenuity and lean times. It can be made from inexpensive ingredients pretty much always available, including overripe (and often plentiful in the South) tomatoes. And its tangy flavors really heighten other recipes that may need a little bit of a boost. Try it over rice or biscuits, for instance. My recipe is a bit different from the traditional because of its smoky flavor.

4 tablespoons (½ stick) salted butter

1 yellow onion, chopped

¼ cup all-purpose flour

1½ cups vegetable broth

1½ cups heavy cream

3 large beefsteak tomatoes, diced

1 teaspoon garlic powder

½ teaspoon cayenne pepper

¼ teaspoon smoked paprika

Kosher salt

Ground black pepper

1. In a medium skillet, melt the butter over medium heat. Add the onions, and cook for 3 to 4 minutes until translucent, stirring constantly. Whisk in the flour until well combined.

2. Whisk in both the broth and the cream. Bring the mixture to a low simmer for 5 minutes, until thickened. Add in the diced tomatoes, garlic, cayenne pepper, paprika, and salt and pepper to taste. Stir together, and allow it to cook for an additional 5 minutes. It should be the consistency of a chunky soup. Remove from heat, and serve while warm.

SUBSTITUTION TIP: For an added smoky flavor, replace the diced fresh tomatoes with 2 (10-ounce) cans of fire-roasted tomatoes.

MAPLE BUTTER SPREAD

Serves 4

Prep time: 10 minutes, plus 1 hour to chill

GLUTEN-FREE, NUT-FREE, SOY-FREE, 5-INGREDIENT

Maple is a staple that connects to the abolition of slavery. The need for cane sugar (production of which used the labor of enslaved individuals) decreased when maple sugar appeared as a less labor-intensive alternative. After the abolition of slavery, the production of cane sugar slowed tremendously and maple sugar filled the hole. This creamy maple butter is simple to make yet adds such a delicate and delightful touch to Sweet Potato Biscuits (page 98) or to my Sticky Gooey Bread Pudding (page 97).

8 tablespoons (1 stick) unsalted butter, softened

¼ cup pure maple syrup

1 teaspoon ground cinnamon

⅛ teaspoon kosher salt

⅛ teaspoon allspice

In a large bowl, combine the butter, maple syrup, cinnamon, salt, and allspice. Mix them together using a whisk or electric mixer. Refrigerate it for at least 1 hour before using. Store it in an airtight container or mason jar in the refrigerator for up to 6 months.

MULTIPURPOSE PIE CRUST

Makes 1 pie crust
Prep time: 10 minutes

DAIRY-FREE, NUT-FREE, VEGAN,
5-INGREDIENT, ONE-PAN, UNDER 30

This pie crust will come in handy for lots of different recipes. Not only is it quick and easy to make, but it also serves as the perfect crust for quiches, pot pies, or dessert pies like Sumptuous Sweet Potato Pie (page 111).

2 cups all-purpose flour

1 teaspoon kosher salt

⅔ cup vegetable
shortening (or unsalted
butter or margarine)

4 tablespoons cold water

1. In a large bowl, combine the flour and salt. Using a pastry cutter or two forks, cut the shortening into the flour. Mix in the water using a fork, and combine until the mixture is moist.

2. Flatten the dough into a baking dish. Fill with pie or other fillings and bake according to the specific recipe.

PREP TIP: Wrapped tightly in plastic wrap, this pie dough can be refrigerated and stored for up to 3 days.

COZY APPLE COBBLER

Serves 8

Prep time: 10 minutes, plus 20 minutes to cool / **Cook time:** 1 hour and 5 minutes

NUT-FREE, SOY-FREE

Although apple pie might be quintessentially American, apple cobbler is quintessentially soul food. The warm, cozy notes of fall mixed with the cinnamon aroma will draw family and friends from far and wide, which explains why this dish is frequently served for big family dinners and holidays like Thanksgiving. My mom passed this cherished recipe down to me.

FOR THE FILLING:

4 tablespoons (½ stick) salted butter

4 pounds Granny Smith apples, peeled and sliced

1 cup packed light brown sugar

½ cup granulated white sugar

¼ cup water

1 tablespoon ground cinnamon

1 tablespoon freshly squeezed lemon juice

½ teaspoon ground nutmeg

1 teaspoon pure vanilla extract

FOR THE CRUST:

2 cups all-purpose flour

1½ cups granulated white sugar

2 teaspoons baking powder

1½ teaspoons ground cinnamon

1 cup (2 sticks) unsalted butter, melted, plus more if needed

1. Preheat the oven to 375°F.

2. **TO MAKE THE FILLING:** In a large skillet, melt the butter over medium heat. Add the apples and stir to cover them in butter. Add the brown sugar, granulated sugar, and water, and cook for 5 minutes while the sugar dissolves, stirring continuously. Add the ground cinnamon, lemon juice, nutmeg, and vanilla. Stir.

3. Allow the apples to cook over medium heat for about 10 more minutes or until they have softened, stirring occasionally. Taste the filling, and add more cinnamon or nutmeg, if desired. Remove from the heat, and pour the apple mixture into a 9-by-13-inch baking dish. Set aside and allow to cool while making the crust.

4. **TO MAKE THE CRUST:** In a large mixing bowl, combine the flour, sugar, baking powder, and cinnamon. Mix thoroughly. Evenly pour this mixture on top of the apple pie filling. Gently pat down and smooth out the flour mixture so that it covers the top. Drizzle the melted butter on top of the flour mixture. Be sure to cover the entire top of the cobbler with melted butter. If there's not enough to cover it, add more.

5. Bake the cobbler in the oven for 40 minutes. If the crust has not browned, continue cooking for an additional 10 minutes or until it is crisp. When done, remove it from the oven, and allow it to cool for at least 20 minutes before serving.

PREP TIP: This dessert is best paired with vanilla ice cream, but you probably didn't need me to tell you that.

PERFECT POUND CAKE

Serves 8

Prep time: 15 minutes, plus 20 minutes to cool / **Bake time:** 1 hour 30 minutes

SOY-FREE, ONE-PAN

Pound cake just like my grandma used to make: that warm, fluffy center with a crispy crust around the edges. There are hundreds of pound cake recipes, including vanilla pound cake, cream cheese pound cake, and lemon pound cake. This pound cake recipe gives you a taste of all three. The cream cheese, lemon, vanilla, almond, and coconut provide the perfect balance.

1½ cups (3 sticks) unsalted butter, softened, plus more for greasing the pan
1 (8-ounce) package cream cheese, softened

3 cups granulated white sugar
6 large eggs
1 tablespoon finely grated lemon zest
1 teaspoon pure vanilla extract

1 teaspoon almond extract
½ teaspoon coconut extract
3 cups all-purpose flour
⅛ teaspoon kosher salt

1. Preheat the oven to 300°F. Grease a Bundt pan with butter.

2. In the bowl of a stand mixer (or a large mixing bowl) combine the butter and cream cheese. Beat at medium speed for 3 minutes or until smooth. Gradually add the sugar, and beat for 5 minutes. Add the eggs one at a time, mixing until each yolk is blended. Then add the lemon zest and the vanilla, almond, and coconut extracts, and blend until combined.

3. In a separate mixing bowl, mix the flour and salt together before slowly adding them into the butter mixture, beating at a low speed until well blended.

4. Pour the batter into the prepared Bundt pan. Bake for 1½ hours or until golden brown. Allow it to cool for 20 minutes on a wire rack before removing the cake from the Bundt pan.

PREP TIP: Place an oven-safe pot filled with 2 cups of water beside the cake during baking to retain moisture. This prevents the cake from drying out. This method to retain moisture can be used for other cake recipes as well.

IMPECCABLE PECAN PIE

Serves 8

Prep time: 5 minutes, plus 20 minutes to cool / **Cook time:** 1 hour

However you may pronounce it—pee-CAN, pe-KAHN, or puh-KAHN—this dish is the pinnacle of desserts to so many Southern families. Living in Georgia for a little over four years allowed me the opportunity to experience pecan pie using some of the freshest pecans. This dish graces menus in many Southern restaurants year-round, and can be found on thousands of dining tables for Thanksgiving and Christmas. To take this dish to the next level, top with a dollop of homemade whipped cream.

1¾ cups granulated white sugar

¼ cup light corn syrup

4 tablespoons (½ stick) salted butter

2 teaspoons cornstarch

1 tablespoon cold water

3 large eggs, beaten

2 cups pecans

2 teaspoons pure vanilla extract

Multipurpose Pie Crust (page 105) or 1 (9-inch) store-bought unbaked pie crust

1. Preheat the oven to 350°F.

2. In a small saucepan, combine the sugar, corn syrup, and butter, and whisk together over medium heat.

3. In a small mixing bowl, prepare a slurry by mixing the cornstarch and water together. Add this slurry to the saucepan with the sugar mixture. Bring the sauce to a boil. When it begins to boil, remove it from the heat.

4. Whisk the beaten eggs into the cooked sauce mixture. When it is thoroughly mixed, add the pecans and vanilla, and stir together. When the mixture is smooth, pour it into the pie crust.

5. Bake for 50 minutes, until the pecans are toasted and the pie is brown. Remove, and allow the pie to cool for at least 20 minutes before enjoying.

BANANA PUDDING SOUTHERN STYLE

Serves 8

Prep time: 10 minutes, plus 2 hours to chill

ONE-PAN

No one really knows how or why banana pudding is such a Southern dessert icon; they just know that it is. This recipe includes a creamy textured pudding, fresh bananas, and melt-in-your-mouth cookies. Originally, banana pudding was made with sponge cake, but with the advent of vanilla wafers (and Nabisco actually placing the recipe on the side of its Nilla Wafers box), vanilla wafers replaced sponge cake as the top choice. Over the years, the recipe has changed in many ways to accommodate shortcuts, like pudding instead of custard, and whipped topping instead of homemade whipped cream. And because it is so convenient to make, it lands on many a holiday table in the South. If my mother does not get a chance to make it for a holiday, one of my sisters always steps in to deliver.

2 cups whole milk, cold

1 (5-ounce) box instant vanilla pudding mix

1 (14-ounce) can sweetened condensed milk

1 (8-ounce) container whipped topping

2 tablespoons pure vanilla extract

1 (11- to 12-ounce) box vanilla wafers (Nabisco Nilla Wafers preferred)

8 large ripe bananas, peeled and sliced

1. In a medium mixing bowl, whisk together the milk and pudding mix until thick. Add the condensed milk, and mix together. Fold in about ¾ of the container of whipped topping and the vanilla. Taste the mixture, and if it is too heavy, fold in the remaining whipped topping.

2. In a serving bowl, create several layers of the pudding mixture, then the vanilla wafers, and then the banana slices until there are none left. Refrigerate for at least 2 hours, and enjoy.

SUBSTITUTION TIP: In recent years, sliced strawberries have been added to banana pudding for extra flavor and sweetness. Feel free to add layers of sliced strawberries to the mix.

SUMPTUOUS SWEET POTATO PIE

Serves 8

Prep time: 10 minutes, plus 40 minutes to cool / **Cook time:** 1 hour and 30 minutes

NUT-FREE

Sweet potato pie is a soul food stalwart. Always popular, it was originally deemed to be a dessert for special occasions because of the process required to make it. It needed an oven for baking, which many enslaved individuals could not access, so it was only cooked in the "big house." After the abolishment of slavery, this pie became more common for African American families. Between the availability of sweet potatoes and increasing access to ovens for baking, it took its place as one of the most popular desserts.

2 medium sweet potatoes

2 large eggs, beaten, room temperature

1 cup granulated white sugar

8 ounces evaporated milk

6 tablespoons (¾ stick) salted butter, melted

¼ cup packed light brown sugar

3 teaspoons ground cinnamon

2 tablespoons self-rising flour

1 teaspoon pure vanilla extract

½ teaspoon nutmeg

¼ teaspoon lemon extract

⅛ teaspoon ground ginger

Multipurpose Pie Crust (page 105) or 1 (9-inch) store-bought unbaked pie crust

1. Preheat the oven to 400°F.

2. On a baking sheet covered in parchment paper, bake the sweet potatoes for 45 minutes. Remove them from the oven, and reduce the oven temperature to 350°F.

3. Let the potatoes cool for 20 minutes. Once cooled, peel the skins. In a large mixing bowl, use an electric mixer to mix the sweet potatoes for 4 minutes or until smooth.

4. In the bowl with the sweet potatoes, add the eggs, granulated sugar, evaporated milk, butter, brown sugar, cinnamon, flour, vanilla, nutmeg, lemon extract, and ground ginger. Whisk into the blended sweet potatoes until smooth and well combined. Taste and add additional sugar, if necessary.

5. Pour the mixture into the pie crust, and bake for 45 minutes or until golden brown. Allow it to cool completely, about 20 minutes, before serving.

SOULFUL PEACH COBBLER

Serves 8

Prep time: 10 minutes, plus 20 minutes to cool / **Cook time:** 1 hour and 5 minutes

NUT-FREE, SOY-FREE

This is one of the most popular soul food desserts across the South. It consists of a warm, tangy, sweet center and a buttery-flaky crust. The peaches used in this recipe can be either fresh or frozen. Fresh peaches are best when picked between May and August. When out of season, it is best to use frozen peaches, which were picked at their peak of freshness. This recipe is all about the peaches, so they need to be tip-top.

FOR THE FILLING:

4 tablespoons (½ stick) salted butter

4 cups peeled and sliced peaches, fresh (from about 6 peaches) or frozen

1 cup packed light brown sugar

½ cup granulated white sugar

2 tablespoons freshly squeezed lemon juice

½ tablespoon ground cinnamon

1 teaspoon pure vanilla extract

½ teaspoon ground nutmeg

FOR THE CRUST:

1 cup all-purpose flour

1 cup granulated white sugar

1 teaspoon baking powder

1 cup whole milk

8 tablespoons (1 stick) unsalted butter, melted

1 tablespoon cinnamon sugar, for topping

1. Preheat the oven to 350°F.

2. **TO MAKE THE FILLING:** In a large pot or skillet, melt the butter over medium heat. Add the peaches, and cook for 10 minutes. Add the brown sugar, granulated sugar, lemon juice, cinnamon, vanilla, and nutmeg. Stir until well combined, and bring to a low simmer for 5 minutes. Taste the sauce, adjust spices and sugars to taste, and remove it from the heat.

3. **TO MAKE THE CRUST:** In a medium mixing bowl, whisk together the flour, sugar, and baking powder thoroughly. Slowly add in the milk, whisking continuously. The batter should be very loose.

4. Pour the melted butter in a 13-by-9-inch casserole dish, then pour the pie crust batter on top, starting from the middle of the dish.

5. Spoon in the peach filling, including the juices. Sprinkle with cinnamon sugar. Bake for 50 minutes until the crust is golden brown. Let it cool for 20 minutes before serving.

MEASUREMENT CONVERSIONS

VOLUME EQUIVALENTS	U.S. STANDARD	U.S. STANDARD (OUNCES)	METRIC (APPROXIMATE)
LIQUID	2 tablespoons	1 fl. oz.	30 mL
	¼ cup	2 fl. oz.	60 mL
	½ cup	4 fl. oz.	120 mL
	1 cup	8 fl. oz.	240 mL
	1½ cups	12 fl. oz.	355 mL
	2 cups or 1 pint	16 fl. oz.	475 mL
	4 cups or 1 quart	32 fl. oz.	1 L
	1 gallon	128 fl. oz.	4 L
DRY	⅛ teaspoon	—	0.5 mL
	¼ teaspoon	—	1 mL
	½ teaspoon	—	2 mL
	¾ teaspoon	—	4 mL
	1 teaspoon	—	5 mL
	1 tablespoon	—	15 mL
	¼ cup	—	59 mL
	⅓ cup	—	79 mL
	½ cup	—	118 mL
	⅔ cup	—	156 mL
	¾ cup	—	177 mL
	1 cup	—	235 mL
	2 cups or 1 pint	—	475 mL
	3 cups	—	700 mL
	4 cups or 1 quart	—	1 L
	½ gallon	—	2 L
	1 gallon	—	4 L

OVEN TEMPERATURES

FAHRENHEIT	CELSIUS (APPROXIMATE)
250°F	120°C
300°F	150°C
325°F	165°C
350°F	180°C
375°F	190°C
400°F	200°C
425°F	220°C
450°F	230°C

WEIGHT EQUIVALENTS

U.S. STANDARD	METRIC (APPROXIMATE)
½ ounce	15 g
1 ounce	30 g
2 ounces	60 g
4 ounces	115 g
8 ounces	225 g
12 ounces	340 g
16 ounces or 1 pound	455 g

INDEX

ACKNOWLEDGMENTS

I have to start by thanking my amazing husband, Cordairo. From reading early drafts and helping me sort through my recipes to playing a major role in recipe testing (tasting), he was there to help me throughout the entire process. I could not have completed this without his support, so to my husband, thank you.

Pharessa, my mother, deserves so much recognition. Without her sharing her love of cooking and recipes, I would not have made it to this step in my journey. She was there from day one of the writing process, assisting with choosing recipes, sorting the recipe list, and providing details of our family history. I can't thank you enough.

To my niece, Deaja, I am so grateful. I could not have made it through the final stages of the writing process without her. She has been extremely supportive and endured late nights just to ensure that my work was complete. No matter the day or hour, she was available to assist selflessly. Her support during this process did not go unnoticed.

To my siblings, remaining family, and friends, I truly appreciate your unwavering support, love, and patience shown throughout this process. Completing such a major project required my full attention, so I thank you all for bearing with me as I worked through it.

ABOUT THE AUTHOR

Alexia Wilkerson is best known as "Just Lexx." She was born and raised in Durham, North Carolina, but currently resides and thrives in Atlanta, Georgia. Her grandmother instilled in her what it means to be family oriented through yearly family reunions, Sunday dinners, and holiday meals. She fell in love with cooking starting around age five, as she watched her mother cook and bake for holidays and special occasions. Her passion for food and cooking continued to grow as she traveled the world, tasting different cuisines and experiencing various techniques. But soul food will always hold a special place for her.

Cooking is Alexia's form of self-expression. Growing up in the South, a lot of this comes through soul food, decadent desserts, and seasoned-to-perfection recipes. Food is universal, and she loves being able to connect with people through her recipes. In May 2020, she created a YouTube channel (Just Lexx), and decided to use it as a creative outlet to share cooking tutorials. Her current goal is to release a series of cookbooks to reach people all around the world, starting right here.

CPSIA information can be obtained
at www.ICGtesting.com
Printed in the USA
JSHW061429240223
38029JS00002B/6